Pride's Crossing

PRIDE'S
CROSSING

TINA HOWE

THEATRE COMMUNICATIONS GROUP

ISBN   1-56865-918-0

Cover Photo of Cherry Jones from the Lincoln Center Theater
production is by Ken Howard
Cover Design by Carol Devine Carson
Test Design and Composition by Lisa Govan

For Madeline B. Post

A h, the lure of playwriting.
    We get to spread our fantasies all over the stage and then invite an audience in to share them. The power, the ecstasy.

Think of it—you're one of two sisters: the ugly one who lives under the porch with the field mice. All your life you've dreamed of being someone—a pilot, a healer, a fabulous beauty. So you create a dazzling alter ego, hire the most radiant actress in the land and put her on stage. She breaks hearts and the sound barrier with a toss of her head. Everyone swoons, but no one more than you because *you* know your place is under the porch. With the field mice.

Or maybe you transform someone else—a friend who's languishing in the hospital or an aging relative. You wrap a turban around their head and drop them in the middle of the desert to found a new religion. It's no wonder we call these labors "plays."

I'm always surprised when people ask if my plays are true. The joy of the theatre comes from *knowing* you're being tricked and surrendering to the deceit. In real life, Nora wouldn't have the nerve to walk out on Torvald, just as Mary Tyrone wouldn't have the presence of mind to come down the stairs, trailing her wedding dress. Characters on stage make entrances and exits we'd never attempt.

There *was* a young woman who swam the English Channel in 1926. A New Yorker named Gertrude Ederle. She was only nineteen and she beat every record on the books. Her time was an astonishing fourteen hours and thirty-nine minutes. This play is not about her, but is inspired by my ninety-year-old Aunt Maddy who never left home, never married and never swam a stroke. So, where's the truth?

For some time now I've wanted to write about the passion of old ladies. When men age, they just get older, but women become very powerful. It's the female thing: that we bear children and nurture the family. As time passes, the membranes between what we *should* do and what we *want* to do get thinner and thinner. There's no rage like old lady rage, just as there's no tenderness like old lady tenderness.

As this century comes to a close, I wanted to celebrate the life of a woman who lived through most of it. I chose my Aunt Maddy because she grew up in a household where women were expected to live under the porch. It was a grand porch, but their place was definitely beneath it. With the field mice. Some women managed to scramble free, but most didn't, so, this is replay for my beloved aunt. This time she rises like a phoenix above the porch, house, shoreline and all.

Tina Howe
New York City
April 1998

PRIDE'S CROSSING

PRODUCTION HISTORY

The world premiere of *Pride's Crossing* was presented by the Old Globe Theatre in January 1997. It was directed by Jack O'Brien. Sets were designed by Ralph Funicello, costumes by Robert Morgan, lights by Michael Gilliam and music and sound by Jeff Ladman. The cast was as follows:

MABEL TIDINGS BIGELOW	Cherry Jones
VITA BRIGHT, PRU O'NEILL, KITTY LOWELL	Marceline Hugot
CHANDLER COFFIN, PHINEAS TIDINGS, MARY O'NEILL	Jeffrey Hayenga
WEST BRIGHT, FRAZIER TIDINGS, PINKY WHEELOCK, DAVID BLOOM	Robert Knepper
GUS TIDINGS, ANTON GUREVITCH, PORTER BIGELOW, WHEELS WHEELOCK	William Anton
MAUD TIDINGS, JULIA RENOIR	Monique Fowler
MINTY RENOIR, EMMA BIGELOW	Hilary Elizabeth Clarke, Nichole Danielle Givans

The New York premiere of *Pride's Crossing* was presented by the Linclon Center Theater in December 1997. It was directed by Jack O'Brien. Sets were designed by Ralph Funicello, costumes by Robert Morgan, lighting by Kenneth Posner, music and sound by Mark Bennett and projections by Jan Hartley. The cast was as follows:

MABEL TIDINGS BIGELOW	Cherry Jones
VITA BRIGHT, PHINEAS TIDINGS, PRU O'NEILL, KITTY LOWELL	Angie Phillips
CHANDLER COFFIN, MARY O'NEILL, DR. PEABODY	Dylan Baker
WEST BRIGHT, FRAZIER TIDINGS, PINKY WHEELOCK, DAVID BLOOM	David Lansbury
GUS TIDINGS, ANTON GUREVITCH, PORTER BIGELOW, WHEELS WHEELOCK	Casey Biggs
MAUD TIDINGS, JULIA RENOIR	Kandis Chappell
MINTY RENOIR, EMMA BIGELOW	Julia McIlvaine

CHARACTERS

MABEL TIDINGS BIGELOW	*A swimmer*
VITA BRIGHT	*Mabel's housekeeper*
CHANDLER COFFIN	*An old friend of Mabel's*
WEST BRIGHT	*Vita's son*
GUS TIDINGS	*Mabel's father*
MAUD TIDINGS	*Mabel's mother*
FRAZIER TIDINGS	*Mabel's brother*
PHINEAS TIDINGS	*Mabel's brother*
JULIA RENOIR	*Mabel's granddaughter*
MINTY RENOIR	*Julia's daughter*
MARY O'NEILL	*The Tidings's cook*
PRU O'NEILL	*The Tidings's serving girl and Mary's daughter*
ANTON GUREVITCH	*Conductor of the Boston Symphony Orchestra*
PORTER BIGELOW	*Mabel's husband*
EMMA BIGELOW	*Mabel's daughter*
KITTY LOWELL	*An old friend of Mabel's*
PINKY WHEELOCK	*An old friend of Mabel's*
WHEELS WHEELOCK	*Pinky's husband*
DR. PEABODY	*A Unitarian minister*
DAVID BLOOM	*A Doctor and swimmer*

AUTHOR'S NOTE

The settings of the scenes are described in considerable detail to give the reader a feeling for the world of the play. This does not mean one has to be a slave to reality, however. Interpretation is all in the theatre, particularly with a memory play. When the director, Jack O'Brien, and the set designer, Ralph Funicello, began discussing the set for the play's premiere at the Old Globe Theatre in January 1997, they came up with a dreamscape of gauze panels and floating windows. There was a minimum of clutter. A Westminster clock hung in midair and that was about it. The presence of food was mimed and there were no croquet balls or broken teacups, just sound effects.

The changes of time and place were accomplished largely through lighting and sound. The projectionist, Jan Hartley, added images of clouds and water when the play was restaged at Lincoln Center Theater. The fluidity of the production was further enhanced by Cherry Jones doing many of her costume changes on stage, in full view of the audience.

The play ends with Mabel wading into the Channel to begin her swim. Miss Jones would have none of it: "I want to *dive*!" she said. "I want to dive into the arms of my fellow actors!"

Because of her daring and Jack's artistry, a thrilling moment of theatre was created. I trust that future readers will indulge in similar flights of fancy as they reenact Mabel's journey.

One more thing—back in the old days when children from these families called their parents "ma*ma*" and "pa*pa*," the accent was always on the second syllable creating an aristocratic flourish.

ACT ONE

Scene 1

The present. A darkened bedroom in the coach house of the former Tidings's estate in Pride's Crossing, Massachusetts. Two twin beds dominate the room. One is piled high with dirty laundry, books, assorted mail and a breakfast tray. Ninety-year-old Mabel Bigelow, wearing a mismatched skirt and blouse, shuffles toward the other bed with the aid of a walker. She collapses onto it with a sigh. It's ten in the morning on a Saturday in the last week of June. Mabel stares into space, then suddenly comes to life.

MABEL: I'm giving a Fourth of July croquet party no matter what anyone says! One has to pass these things down. I was quite the player in my day. Minty has probably never laid eyes on a croquet mallet. Poor child . . . Growing up half way around the world in Paris. I don't approve. I don't approve at all.

(Vita Bright, a hippie-type woman dressed as Paul Revere comes galloping in as if on horseback. She's in her thirties.)

VITA: "The British are coming, the British are coming!"
MABEL: Help, helllllp . . .
VITA:
"One, if by land and two if by sea,
And I on the opposite shore will be."

MABEL (*Reaching for her phone and dialing*): 911? This is Mabel Bigelow on Hale Street. A maniac has just broken into my house!

VITA: It's me, your housekeeper, *Vita Bright*!

MABEL (*With a laugh*): Vita, Vita . . . I knew it was you all along!

(*Silence as Mabel takes her in.*)

MABEL: And what are you doing in that extraordinary outfit, if I may ask?

VITA: I'm going to be Paul Revere in the Fourth of July parade.

MABEL: Speak up, speak up!

VITA: I said: I'M GOING TO LEAD THE PARADE AS PAUL REVERE ON THE FOURTH OF JULY!

MABEL: But you're a *woman*.

VITA: So?

MABEL: You should go as Betsy Ross or Martha Washington.

VITA: But they're so boring.

MABEL: They are boring!

VITA: Men have all the fun.

MABEL: Men do have all the fun, it's not fair! I often wish I'd been a man.

VITA: I get to ride a horse.

(*Silence as Mabel gazes at her.*)

MABEL: I love your hat!

VITA: Would you like to try it on?

MABEL: *Could* I?

VITA (*Handing it to her*): Be my guest.

MABEL (*Putting it on and striking a pose*):
    "A horse, a horse!
    My kingdom for a horse!"

VITA: Go, Mrs. B.!

MABEL: "Don't shoot till you see the whites of their eyes!"

VITA: We should be allowed to switch genders once in a while.

MABEL: I always wanted to be Charlemagne. Soldier, emperor, scholar . . . There was a life.

VITA *(Picking it up)*: Here, let me get rid of your breakfast tray.

MABEL: Darling Vita, what would I do without you?

VITA *(Exiting)*: I shudder to think.

(Mabel gazes into space for several moments and then surveys the mountain of stuff on the other bed. She picks up a bill.)

MABEL: A hundred and eight dollars? How could my phone bill be a hundred and eight dollars? I never talk to a soul. What's this? A dividend from State Street! *(She kisses it)* God bless State Street and my piddling income. I shudder to think where I'd be without it. In the street, in the street. *(She picks up another bill)* The Beverly Visiting Nurse Service? Eight hundred and thirty-three dollars? What next? *(She stuffs it at the bottom of the pile and sinks back onto the pillows, exhausted. A moment passes)* VIIIIITAAA? OH, VIIIIIITAAA?

VITA *(From offstage)*: You called?

MABEL: Could I trouble you for a glass of water, please? I'm parched.

VITA: Coming right up.

MABEL: DARLING VITA . . . YOU'RE MY GUARDIAN ANGEL, MY KNIGHT IN SHINING ARMOR, MY FLORENCE . . . *(Struggling to remember)* FLORENCE . . . *(She starts singing)* "You are my lucky star . . . something something, my heart's desire . . ."

VITA *(Returning with a glass of water)*: Here you go.

MABEL: Thank you, thank you.

(She drinks deeply and then makes a lurid kissing sound.)

VITA *(Picking up a bottle of pills)*: Did you take your pills?

MABEL: Pay my bills?

VITA: NO, TAKE YOUR PILLS!

MABEL: You have such lovely skin.

VITA: Don't change the subject. Where's your ear?

MABEL: If I'd had skin like that, just think what I could have accomplished.

VITA: I SAID, "WHERE'S YOUR EAR?"

MABEL: I don't know.

VITA: *You don't know?*

MABEL: Don't scold me, I can't stand being scolded.

VITA: HOW MANY TIMES DO I HAVE TO TELL YOU? YOU SHOULD PUT IT ON YOUR BEDSIDE TABLE . . .

MABEL	VITA:
(Covering her ears):	
Ba, ba, ba, ba, ba, ba,	THAT WAY YOU KNOW
ba, ba, ba, ba, ba, ba,	WHERE IT IS WHEN YOU
ba, ba, ba, ba, ba, ba.	NEED IT AGAIN!

(Silence.)

MABEL: Wait till you're ninety!

VITA: If you just took more responsibility for yourself, it would make life so much easier. You swam the English Channel, after all.

MABEL: Any fool can swim the English Channel, all it takes is endurance.

VITA: Plus a few other attributes like talent and skill.

MABEL *(Rummaging around the other bed)*: Damn ear . . . God, I hate this!

VITA *(Finding it)*: Your audiological device, madame!

(Mabel pops it in her ear. It makes a loud whine.)

VITA: Turn it down, turn it down!

(The front doorbell rings. Vita exits to answer it.)

MABEL: Where are you going?

VITA: Someone's at the door.

MABEL: Then go answer it.

VITA *(Offstage)*: Mr. Coffin . . .

MABEL: WHO IS IT?

VITA *(To Mabel)*: MR. COFFIN!

MABEL *(Calling out)*: HI. CHAN!

CHANDLER: HI, M. T.!

> *(To Vita)* Mrs. Bigelow said she wanted to see me. That it was urgent.

MABEL *(To Chandler)*: WHAT ARE YOU DOING HERE?

CHANDLER *(To Vita)*: How is she?

VITA: Impossible! Come in, come in . . .

> *(Vita ushers in Chandler Coffin. He's several years older than Mabel and walks with a severe limp. He's the picture of old-world elegance, dressed in a cream-colored suit and jaunty Panama hat from the twenties.)*

MABEL: Look at you! You're a vision, a vision!

CHANDLER:

> "An aged man is but a paltry thing,
> A tattered coat upon a stick."
>
> Yeats.
>
> *(A pause as he takes Mabel in)* What an extraordinary hat!

MABEL: Isn't it divine?

CHANDLER: You look like Paul Revere.

VITA: You *knew*, you *knew*!

MABEL: It's part of Vita's Fourth of July costume.

CHANDLER: "Listen my children, and you shall hear . . ."

CHANDLER AND VITA: "Of the midnight ride of Paul Revere . . ."

CHANDLER: Longfellow.

MABEL: Nicely done.

> *(To Chandler)* And to what do I owe the pleasure?

CHANDLER: You called and insisted I come over right away.

MABEL: I did?

CHANDLER: You said it was urgent. Something about a croquet party.

VITA: A croquet party?

MABEL *(Glancing at Vita)*: Shhh, not so loud.

VITA: What's this about a croquet party?

MABEL: Alright, Vita, you may go now.

VITA: You know what the doctor said. No entertaining or you could bring on another stroke.

MABEL: *I said, that will be all!*

VITA: Remember what happened at last year's party. The fire department had to rush you to the Beverly hospital

MABEL *(Whacking the bed with her cane)*: You heard me. Out, out, out!

(Vita scurries out of the room. Silence.)

CHANDLER: I've never seen that woman in a pair of shoes.

MABEL: Affordable live-ins are as scarce as hen's teeth, I'm lucky to have her.

CHANDLER: But she's got that awful son, West. I heard he almost went to jail.

MABEL: He's not so bad.

CHANDLER: You're more tolerant than I am.

MABEL: Well, I had children and you didn't. Though my daughter Emma hasn't spoken to me in years.

CHANDLER: How *is* Emma?

MABEL: I have no idea! Poor thing . . . She was doomed from the start. Always seeking her reflection in the bottom of a glass . . . Just like her father. I practically raised her daughter, Julia.

(Pointing to a chaise strewn with undergarments) Sit down, sit down, take a load off your feet.

(Chandler heads for the chaise, but stops seeing her underthings.)

MABEL: It's just my darning. Shove it to one side, it won't bite.

(Chandler gingerly moves a ratty bra.)

MABEL *(Laughing)*: Poor Chan . . .

CHANDLER *(Sitting down)*: You sound just like my mother. *(In her voice)* "Poor Chan . . ." She always said my name as if I had a terminal illness. Now what's all this about a croquet party?

MABEL: Julia's coming tomorrow. My favorite grandchild, my *only* grandchild who deigns to visit me. She only comes once a year, if that.

CHANDLER: She lives in Paris.

MABEL: Oh well, beggars can't be choosers.

CHANDLER: Julia's devoted to you, and you know it.

MABEL: She'll be staying through the Fourth of July.

CHANDLER: How nice.

MABEL: So I'm planning a croquet party like Mama and Papa used to have in the old days.

CHANDLER: Not so fast . . .

MABEL: I stumbled across some of Grandmother's heavenly old lawn dresses the ladies can wear for the occasion.

CHANDLER: And where will you have this grand croquet party, pray tell?

MABEL: In the backyard, of course.

CHANDLER: But it's a wilderness out there.

MABEL: That's why I asked you over. To discuss hiring Isobel Sargent's yard man to spruce it up.

CHANDLER: M. T., M. T. . . .

MABEL: She's wild about him!

CHANDLER: It would take more than Isobel's yard man to fix up that yard.

MABEL: He's strong as an ox and has lovely manners.

CHANDLER: We're talking a level playing field, a hundred and five by eighty-four feet.

MABEL: That's why I need him so badly!

CHANDLER: I thought you were having money problems.

MABEL *(Angry)*: OH, STOP BEING SUCH AN OLD MAID, FOR GOD'S SAKE! IT'S NO WONDER YOU'RE ALL ALONE IN THE WORLD!

(An awful silence.)

MABEL: I'm sorry, that was cruel.

CHANDLER: But why a *croquet* party? No one plays croquet anymore.

MABEL: Well, they should, it's great fun.

CHANDLER: It was fun in your parents' day because they had the grounds for it.

MABEL: We could use a little fun around here.

CHANDLER: Times have changed. You're living in the chauffeur's cottage.

MABEL: So?

CHANDLER: There's no room!

MABEL: I've already drawn up the guest list, so there!

CHANDLER: I'm not listening to this!

MABEL *(Miraculously producing it)*: You, Kitty Lowell, Isobel Sargent, Gabby Ames and the doddering Wheelocks . . . if they're still alive.

CHANDLER: You are not, I repeat, not giving a Fourth of July party or any other party. End of discussion!

(West Bright, Vita's son, charges into the room. He's around fifteen and has just been in a fight. His clothes are torn and his hands and face are bleeding.)

WEST: *Mom, Mom! Where's Mom?*

MABEL:	CHANDLER:
Good grief!	West!

WEST *(Near tears)*: STUPID ASSHOLES!

VITA *(Rushing into the room)*: Not again . . .

WEST: SONS OF BITCHES!

VITA *(Grabbing him by the shoulders)*: What happened?

WEST *(Wrenching away from her)*: I'M GOING TO KILL THEM, I'M GOING TO KILL THEM!

CHANDLER: Easy, son, easy . . .

MABEL: He's bleeding, call a doctor!

VITA: Westie, Westie, why are you always fighting?

WEST: Like *I* start it . . .

VITA: Well, you usually do.

WEST: That's right, take their side.

CHANDLER: Calm down, son.

WEST: Mind your own business and stop calling me "son"!

VITA *(Reaching for West)*: Honey . . .

WEST *(Whirling away from her)*: Don't touch me!

VITA: But you're bleeding.

WEST: I said, *don't touch me!*

CHANDLER: I don't like the look of that hand.

WEST *(To Chandler)*: Fuck off, asshole!

CHANDLER *(Reeling as if struck)*: I beg your pardon?

WEST: I said, outta my face, *asshole!*

VITA: Apologize to Mr. Coffin right this minute.

WEST: Make me!

VITA: I don't believe this!

MABEL *(Whacking her cane on the bottom of her bed)*: THAT'S IT, EVERYBODY OUT! I'M TRYING TO PLAN A PARTY HERE AND AM GETTING NO COOPERATION! YOU CAN'T COME CHARGING IN HERE LIKE YOU OWN THE PLACE!

(No one moves.)

MABEL: YOU HEARD ME . . . OUT, OUT! AND THAT INCLUDES YOU, CHAN! YOU'RE TREATING ME LIKE A CHILD AND I WON'T HAVE IT, I TELL YOU, I WON'T!

(Fragments of their angry words dovetail into another argument Mabel witnessed some eighty years before.)

SCENE 2

The dining room of the Tidings's spacious summer house that perches above the Atlantic. The year is 1917. It's shortly before nine on a Saturday morning in June and the family is gathered around the table having breakfast. The room is formal and imposing. Family portraits and paintings of sailing ships adorn the walls. Gus Tidings, mid-forties, sits at the head of the table. He's dressed in natty sailing gear and is in a towering rage. He's flanked by his sons: Phineas, eighteen; and Frazier, sixteen. They're also dressed for sailing. Gus's wife Maud sits across from him, her hair swept up in an elegant Gibson knot. She's in her mid-thirties and is fighting a migraine. She wears an austere high-necked, long-sleeved dress. Mabel, ten, wears a starched pinafore. She sits next to Frazier who's very red in the face.

FRAZIER: I just drove it around the driveway.

GUS: You know the rules . . .

MAUD: Someone could have gotten hurt.

GUS: *No one drives my car!*

FRAZIER: Except Phineas.

GUS: Oh, really?

MAUD: You're only sixteen.

FRAZIER: You let Phinney drive it when he was thirteen.

(Phinney guiltily looks down at his plate.)

GUS: Do tell.

MAUD: You could have lost control and plunged into the ocean.

FRAZIER: You encouraged him.

GUS: I thought I just said no one drives my car.

MAUD: I can see the headlines now: "AUGUSTUS TIDINGS'S CAR PULLED OUT OF THE ATLANTIC. HIS SON, FRAZIER, FOUND DEAD AT THE WHEEL."

FRAZIER: You waved at him from the porch.

GUS: I waved at him from the porch?

MABEL *(Trying to restrain him)*: Frazier, don't . . .

FRAZIER: I remember it as clear as day.

GUS: This is getting better and better.

FRAZIER: You took off your hat and waved.

MABEL *(Pulling at Frazier)*: Stop it, you're making Papa angry.

FRAZIER: But I *saw* you!

GUS: It's bad enough you drove the car, now you're contradicting me!

FRAZIER: Every time he circled the driveway, you waved him on, shouting, "*That's* my boy!" *(He stands, mimicking it)* "That's *my* boy, that's my *boy* . . ." *(He keeps it up)*

MAUD *(Passing her hands over her eyes)*: Frazier, please!

GUS *(Rising from his chair)*: ENOUGH IS ENOUGH, GO TO YOUR ROOM!

MAUD: He's impossible.

GUS *(Banging the table with his fist)*: NOW!

FRAZIER *(With rising intensity)*: "*That's* my boy, that's *my* boy, that's my *boy*, that's my . . ."

MAUD: Just like my father. It's in the blood.

GUS: I said *GO!* *(He hurls a glass across the room. It shatters)*

(Silence.)

MAUD *(Wincing in pain)*: *Plus ça change, plus c'est la même chose.*

FRAZIER *(Bowing deeply, doffing an imaginary hat)*: Sir, madame, Phineas, Mabel . . . I take my leave.

GUS: AND THERE'LL BE NO COMMODORE'S RACE FOR YOU TODAY!

FRAZIER: Who said I wanted to go? I'd rather drink blood than go sailing with you.

MABEL *(Near tears)*: He doesn't mean it, he doesn't mean it.

FRAZIER *(Exiting)*: I hope the boat capsizes and you both drown.

MAUD: Apologize to your father right this minute.

FRAZIER *(Pausing at the door)*: Slowly. Very. Slowly. *(He exits)*

(Silence. The Westminster mantel clock starts striking nine.)

MAUD *(With forced good cheer)*: Alright, children, eat up, eat up. Your eggs are getting cold.

(No one moves.)

GUS: Well, Phinney, it looks like it'll be just you and me.

PHINNEY: Aye, aye, sir.

GUS: That's my boy. We're going to win this race.

PHINNEY: Here, here.

MAUD: Mary's packing you a lunch.

GUS: Nothing too fancy, I trust. *(Winking)* A little caviar, some cold lobster, a few bottles of champagne . . .

MAUD: Now, now . . .

PHINNEY: Sounds good to me.

MAUD: You want to cross the finish line, not sink underneath it.

GUS: And who's *won* the Challenger's Cup for the past five years?

MAUD: I don't like you drinking when you sail.

GUS: My dear Maud, are you insinuating . . .

MAUD: Remember what happened last week. *(She passes her hand over her eyes again)*

MABEL: Are you alright, Mama?

MAUD: It's just one of my headaches.

MABEL: I'm sorry.

MAUD: Where were we? Oh yes, the Commodore's Race.

GUS: We should push off soon, the harbor's going to be jammed. Every Tom, Dick and Harry will be there.

MABEL: May I come?

GUS: *You?*

MABEL: Why not?

MAUD: Good grief, what next?

PHINNEY: It would be good for her.

GUS: This is a serious race, it's no place for children.

MAUD: Especially little girls.

MABEL: I could help.

GUS: What on earth would you *do?*

PHINNEY: Swab the deck, man the bilge . . .

MABEL: Phinney!

PHINNEY: I'm only kidding. You can be the copilot.

MABEL *(Imitating one)*: Hard-a-lee. Coming about, coming about . . .

MAUD: Girls don't sail, it's just not done.

MABEL: Why not?

MAUD: It's not becoming.

MABEL: I can swim.

MAUD: Anybody can swim.

GUS: Boxer can swim.

(Maud and Gus bark and emit hoots of laughter.)

MAUD: Girls belong indoors.

MABEL: Yesterday I made it to Little Misery and back.

GUS *(Patronizing)*: *Little Misery?* I don't believe it!

MABEL: And I wasn't even tired.

PHINNEY: It's true, I was with her. She was like a machine. A paddle wheel or locomotive . . .

MAUD: Don't encourage her!

PHINNEY: She has incredible determination. Remember the time she held her breath for over three minutes?

MAUD (*World-weary*): Mabel, Mabel . . .

MABEL: I'll do it again. Watch . . .

PHINNEY: She passed out before she gave up.

MABEL: Time me, Phin. (*She takes a huge gulp of air*)

PHINNEY: I could never do that.

MAUD: *No playing at the table!*

PHINNEY: For all our daring, divers can't lose control.

GUS: A real swim is crossing the English Channel. A distant relative of mine did it in 1875.

MABEL: Someone *swam* the English Channel?

GUS: Don't they teach you any history at that school?

MAUD: Of course they do. She just doesn't pay attention. She's like you . . . Head in the clouds.

MABEL: How far across is it?

GUS: Twenty-one miles. It's not the distance that's daunting, but the weather. I've never experienced such rough waters. I know, I've sailed them. My father took me the summer I turned fifteen. I've never been so seasick in my life.

GUS, MAUD AND PHINNEY: The entire crew was hanging over the edge of the boat.

MAUD: What possessed you to go?

GUS: It's one of those challenges like climbing Mount Everest. You do it because it's there.

MAUD: The Sahara Desert is there too, but that doesn't mean you have to walk across it.

GUS: I beg to differ.

MAUD: Augustus Tilden Tidings, I'll never understand you as long as I live.

GUS: I don't ask for understanding, just a little tolerance.

(*Silence.*)

MAUD: I'm parched. Who'd like more orange juice? (*She raises the pitcher. No one responds*)

GUS: How old were you when you started to dive, Phin?

MABEL: Ten.

MAUD: How would you know? You weren't even born yet.

MABEL: Yes, I was. I remember watching him dive off the rocks from the nursery.

GUS: Who would have thought our Phineas would end up an Olympic diver?

MAUD: It's not surprising in the least, look what he comes from.

MABEL: He'd stand up so straight and tall. Like an Indian chief. Then he'd lift up on the smalls of his feet . . .

GUS: *Balls* of his feet.

MAUD: Honestly, Mabel!

MABEL: Spread out his arms and leap. I was so surprised when he dropped down, I always expected him to fly.

PHINNEY: Come on, you're embarrassing me.

MABEL: I remember one time, he arched so high I thought . . .

MAUD *(Reaching for Phinney's hand)*: It's true. Watching you dive is like poetry.

GUS: Accept it, Phin, you're the best there is.

MABEL: Better than the best!

(Silence as everyone gazes at him.

Frazier suddenly enters, smeared with fake blood. He sports a loincloth and halo and has several trick arrows stuck in his chest.)

FRAZIER: I'm back!

GUS:	MAUD:	MABEL:	PHINNEY:
Good God!	Frazier!	Fray!	What next?

FRAZIER *(Slouching against the door, mimicking the famous Mantegna painting)*: Saint Sebastian, early Christian martyr.

GUS: What is this?

FRAZIER *(Grabbing Gus's hand and sinking to his knees)*: Have mercy! Let me sail!

(Silence as everyone looks at Gus, waiting for his response.)

GUS *(Finally bursts out laughing)*: Frazier, Frazier . . . You know what I admire about you? You're an original.

MAUD: Just like my father.

GUS: It will either make or destroy you.

MAUD: The most brilliant architect of his day. Statesman, Harvard professor, trustee of the Boston Symphony . . .

ALL: Two minutes before his forty-fifth birthday, he put on a tux, walked into the reading room of the Atheneum, pulled out a revolver and *shot* himself through the heart!

MAUD: The blood had gone bad. Poor Mama never got over it. Widowed at forty-two with three small children.

FRAZIER *(Dropping to his knees)*: Let me sail, I implore you!

GUS: On one condition.

FRAZIER: Anything, anything!

GUS: That you put on some clothes.

FRAZIER: What, you don't like this? *(He strikes outrageous poses, then pulls out the arrows, wipes off the fake blood and offers his halo to Mabel)* Mabel Tidings, step forward please.

MABEL: Who, me?

FRAZIER: Yes, *you*!

(Mabel advances.)

FRAZIER: On your knees.

(Mabel kneels before him.)

FRAZIER: On behalf of the Commonwealth of Massachusetts and all the God-fearing citizens of Pride's Crossing, I hereby give you Saint Sebastian's halo. *(He places it on her head)* Tell me your heart's desire and it will be yours.

MAUD *(World-weary)*: Frazier, Frazier . . .

GUS: He's *your* son, not mine.

MABEL: Anything?

FRAZIER: *Anything!*

GUS *(Looking at his watch)*: Good God, look at the time! *(Heading for the door)* Come on boys, we've got a race to win!

MAUD: I think I'll head back to bed, I'm not feeling well.

PHINNEY *(Tagging Frazier)*: Last one out's a rotten egg!

FRAZIER *(Chasing after him)*: Oh no you don't.

(Phinney and Frazier race for the door, knocking over chairs.)

MAUD: Boys, boys . . .

MABEL: Wait! My wish.

MAUD: You're acting like savages!

PHINNEY *(Scuffling in the hall)*: I won, I won!

FRAZIER: Did not.

PHINNEY: Did so!

FRAZIER: Did not.

PHINNEY: Did so!

MAUD *(To Mabel as she exits)*: Wait till *you're* a mother!

MABEL: What about my wish? Doesn't anybody want to hear my wish? *(Shutting her eyes. With great solemnity)* Someday I'm going to swim the English Channel and be famous like Phinney!

(Light emanates from her halo. It shines brighter and brighter and then snaps out.)

Scene 3

The present. Mabel's living room, around 2:30 the next after-noon. Julia Renoir (Mabel's granddaughter) and Minty Renoir (Julia's daughter) have just arrived. They face her like soldiers on a reviewing stand.

MABEL: Well, finally!

JULIA: Hi, Grand.

MABEL: Don't just stand there. Come give your doddering old grandmother a kiss.

JULIA *(Kissing her cheek)*: Maa!

MABEL: God, you look awful!

JULIA: Thanks a lot.

MABEL: You look a hundred years old.

JULIA: How nice of you to mention it.

MABEL *(Pointing at Minty)*: And who's *that* mysterious creature trying to disappear under the floorboards.

JULIA *(Softly to Minty)*: Give Great Grand a kiss.

MABEL: Don't tell me it's *Minty*!

JULIA: Go on . . .

MABEL: The last time I saw you, you were in diapers.

JULIA: It hasn't been *that* long. *(Pushing Minty toward Mabel)* Kiss Mou-Mou . . .

(Mabel makes her lurid kissing sound. Minty doesn't move.)

JULIA: We're waiting.

(Minty hastily kisses Mabel on both cheeks.)

MABEL: Oh, I love that European style of kissing! Do it again, do it again! *(She makes scary throat-clearing noises)*

(Minty doesn't move.)

JULIA *(Softly to Minty)*: You heard her.
MABEL: Her being able to kiss like that almost makes up for your living so far away.

(Minty doesn't move.)

JULIA: *Vas y, Mignone, ne sois pas si timide!*

(Mabel spits into a tissue. Minty is frozen to the spot.)

JULIA: *Vas y, vas y . . . !*
MABEL: It's alright, let her be.
JULIA *(Getting angrier and angrier)*: *Qu'est-ce-que tu fais, Mignone? Ce n'est pas gentil.*
MABEL: It's alright, let her be.

(Minty hastily kisses her again.)

MABEL: Thank you Minty, that was very brave. *(Pause)* How old are you these days?
MINTY: Ten.
MABEL: *Ten?* I thought you were seventeen!
JULIA: Spare me!
MABEL: Do you remember the last time you were here?
MINTY: Sort of.
JULIA: She was only six.
MINTY: I slept in a funny little room upstairs.
MABEL: The hayloft. This used to be the chauffeur's cottage. And before that it was a stable, if you can believe it. The place was crawling with mice!
MINTY: Ewww, I hate mice!
MABEL: You *do?*
MINTY: They give me the creeps!

MABEL: But they're so cunning.

MINTY: "Cunning"?

JULIA *(To Minty)*: Cute.

MABEL: There's a darling family that lives in the upstairs bathroom. They've built the most charming nest under the sink. It's made out of rags and bits of toilet paper.

MINTY: Ewwww! Ewwww!

MABEL: Wait till you see it . . . It even has a little swing set for the babies . . .

MINTY *(Covering her ears)*: Stop stop . . .

MABEL: I'm just kidding . . . But we do have bats.

MINTY *(Terrified): Bats?*

JULIA *(Heading for the door)*: I'm leaving!

MINTY *(Running after her)*: Wait for me!

MABEL *(Laughing)*: I've never seen such a gullible pair! You'd believe anything!

JULIA *(World-weary)*: Grand, Grand . . .

MABEL: I just love how you call me "Grand"! It makes me sound like an Oriental potentate.

MINTY *(Gazing at Mabel out of shining eyes)*: That was neat!

MABEL *(To Julia)*: I want you to meet Vita, darling. The woman's a saint. I don't know how she puts up with me. *(Calling)* Vita . . . Oh, Vita . . .

VITA *(From offstage)*: Yes?

MABEL *(To Minty, conspiratorially)*: Come on, let's have a little fun. *(To Vita) Come quick, there's a gorilla in the parlor!*

VITA *(From the kitchen)*: A gorilla in the parlor?

MABEL *(Nudging Minty, making little gorilla noises)*: Go on . . .

(Minty lopes around like a gorilla.)

MABEL: Atta girl . . .

JULIA *(Laughing)*: You two . . .

VITA *(Entering, feigning surprise)*: HELLLLLP, A GORILLA!

(Minty gets more and more into it, grunting and beating her chest.)

JULIA: Alright, Minty, that's enough.

MABEL *(Clapping)*: Nicely done, nicely done!

JULIA: I'd forgotten how strenuous these visits are.

MABEL *(To Vita)*: *That* is my great-grandchild, Minty!

VITA: So I gathered. *(She does a quick gorilla turn)*

MINTY: More, more! . . . *(Tries to outdo Vita)*

JULIA: *Ça suffit, petite! S'il te plais!*

(Minty retreats to a chair.)

MABEL *(To Vita)*: And *this* is my granddaughter Julia. *(Introducing them)* Vita Bright . . . Julia Renoir.

JULIA *(Shaking her hand)*: I've heard so much about you.

VITA: Is that *Renoir*, as in the painter?

MABEL: Her husband's a distant relative. How is Jean-Jacques, by the way?

JULIA: Jean-*Paul!*

MABEL: Whatever. Still working like a Trojan?

JULIA: Still working like a Trojan.

MABEL: She's married to the finest heart specialist in Paris.

JULIA: Now, now . . .

MABEL: Well, he is. He's also as handsome as the day is long. I don't trust that man around the corner.

JULIA: Here we go . . .

MABEL: They all have mistresses over there. I have a dim view of good-looking men, in case you haven't noticed.

JULIA: Just because your husband was an alcoholic, doesn't mean—

MABEL: You can't let them out of your sight for a minute, particularly if they're French. *Voulez-vous coucher avec moi ce soir? (She makes her lurid kissing noise)* I've had my adventures with handsome foreign men.

JULIA: The infamous David Bloom.

VITA: *David Bloom?* I've never heard you mention any . . .

JULIA: The dashing Englishman who wanted to run away with her after her swim.

MABEL: Alright Julia, that's enough.

JULIA: Well, he did.

VITA: Go, Mrs. B.!

JULIA: She met him over there while she was training.

MABEL *(Wistful)*: *Porpoise oil!*

VITA: Porpoise oil?

MABEL: He covered me with porpoise oil before I went in. He had the most beautiful hands . . .

JULIA: He was a doctor.

MABEL: Drawn from the water.

VITA: Drawn from the water?

MABEL: That's what Moses means.

JULIA *(Sotto voce to Vita)*: He was Jewish.

VITA *(Pleased)*: Like West's father!

JULIA: And wildly handsome. He did the swim the year before her.

VITA: So, why didn't you go off with him?

MABEL: I don't want to talk about it.

JULIA: Just think, you'd be living in London or Oxford. *(Putting on an accent)* Pip pip and cheerio . . .

MABEL: I SAID I DON'T WANT TO TALK ABOUT IT!

(Silence.)

JULIA: When Jean-Paul asked me to marry him I didn't think twice. Of course he was *French*, and French men are much sexier than English men.

MABEL: Well, Minty, I hope you brought your bathing suit. We're expecting some beautiful weather.

JULIA: The way he looked at me . . . It was as if his eyes had tongues. Of course, that was years ago. Now he barely notices me.

(Silence.)

MABEL *(To Vita)*: Julia's an *architect*, if you can believe it. She just designed some frightfully important museum of arts and crafts behind the Louvre.

JULIA: It's nowhere near the Louvre, it's in Neuilly. And I didn't design it, I'm part of a firm.

MABEL: My grandfather was an architect, you know. He designed half the buildings in Boston. He was a remarkable man.

MABEL AND JULIA: Two minutes before his forty-fifth birthday, he put on a tux, walked into the reading room of the Atheneum, pulled out a revolver and *shot* himself through the heart.

MABEL: The blood had gone bad. Too blue, too thin . . . spent. A condition that plagues most of the old families around here, in case you haven't noticed.

(Silence. The Westminster clock chimes three.)

MINTY: Can I go upstairs and see if there are any mice in my room?

MABEL: You mean, "*May* I go upstairs and see if there are any mice in my room?" Yes, you may. And no there aren't. West already checked. That's *his* department.

(Minty scampers off.)

MABEL *(To Julia)*: She's divine, divine . . .

   (To Vita) Well, don't just stand there, let's get lunch under way before we all keel over with hunger. Vita prepared a veritable feast. All your favorites.

VITA *(Exiting)*: It's hardly a feast. Just shepherd's pie, corn on the cob and apple brown Betty for dessert.

(Silence.)

JULIA *(Pulling up close to Mabel)*: So, how are you?

MABEL: Still breathing.

JULIA: How's your walking?

MABEL: I don't want to talk about it.

JULIA: Do you get outside at all?

MABEL: Julia, Julia, it's so good to see you. How's your wretched mother?

JULIA: Miserable.

MABEL: Poor Emma, what number husband is she on now?

JULIA: Five and don't change the subject.

MABEL: Good God!

JULIA: He's not bad. Dull, but very rich. *(Pause)* Do you get to the beach?

MABEL: Rarely.

JULIA: What about gardening?

MABEL: I haven't pulled up a weed in I don't know how long.

JULIA: It's important to move around.

MABEL: I said, *I don't want to talk about it!* How are things in Paris?

JULIA: In the words of a distant relative of mine, "I don't want to talk about it!"

(Silence.)

MABEL: Well, I hope you're up for some excitement. I'm having a Fourth of July croquet party.

JULIA: Grand, *no!*

MABEL: We could use a little gaiety around here.

JULIA: Why do you always insist on having a party when I come?

MABEL: Because I like them. You never know what's going to happen next. What would you think if your ancient grandmother disappeared into the bushes with Mr. Wheelock or Chandler Coffin?

JULIA: *Grand!*

MABEL: Or better yet, did a spirited jig with the attractive young man who's mowing the lawn?

JULIA: Remember what happened last year? Chandler Coffin told me you had to be rushed to the hospital in a fire truck.

MABEL: And it was great fun. *(She imitates the siren)*

JULIA: For *you!*

MABEL: I love parties, I've always loved parties. They bring out the best in people.

JULIA: Not when they're as frail as you are.

MABEL: That, my love, is when you need them the most. I want to exit with a flourish.

JULIA: *Exit?*

(Vita enters ringing a bell.)

VITA: LUNCH IS READY, LUUUUUNCH!

(Minty lets out a series of piercing screams from upstairs. Vita screams.)

MABEL:	JULIA:
Good God!	Minty, Minty . . .

(Minty runs in hiding something behind her back.)

MINTY: Eww, eww, ewww . . .

JULIA *(Rushing over to her)*: What happened?

MINTY: LOOK! *(She whips out a dead mouse caught in a trap)*

(Vita and Julia scream.)

MINTY: Yuk, yuk!!! *(She drops the mouse in front of Mabel)*

MABEL: Is *that* all?

JULIA: Minty, you nearly gave us a heart attack!

MABEL *(Reaching for it)*: The poor thing is dead. It can't hurt you.

VITA:	JULIA:	MINTY:
Mrs. B.! . . .	*Don't touch it!*	EWWWWWWW!

MABEL *(Picking it up)*: What's dead is dead. There's no com- ing back. *(She releases the mouse from the trap and drops it into a vase)*

(Julia, Vita and Minty shudder, clutching onto each other.)

MABEL: Chop, chop, it's time for lunch. I've never seen such a bunch of scaredy-cats! Lunch, lunch . . .

(Mabel reaches for her walker and starts to rise. She loses her balance and sways on her feet.)

JULIA *(Rushing to her, grabbing her arm)*: Grand!

MABEL *(Whirling away from her)*: DON'T TOUCH ME! IF YOU TOUCH ME, I'LL FALL!

VITA *(Softly to Julia)*: Leave her alone. It's best if she does it herself.

MABEL *(Starts making her way across the room)*:
"Row, row, row your boat,
Gently down the stream . . ."

JULIA *(To Vita)*: She's so much worse.

MABEL:
"Merrily, merrily, merrily, merrily,
Life is but a dream."

VITA: It's the arthritis.

JULIA: She can hardly move.

VITA: What are you talking about? This is a good day, ISN'T IT, MRS. B.?

MABEL: Hmmm?

VITA: I SAID: "THIS IS A GOOD DAY"!

(Mabel turns toward Vita and loses her balance again. She paddles the air.)

JULIA *(Grabbing her arm)*: I've got you!

MABEL *(Wrenching out of her grasp, wild)*: I SAID, DON'T TOUCH ME! WHAT'S THE MATTER, ARE YOU DEAF?! *(She takes several wobbly steps)* Mmmmm, smell that shepherd's pie . . .

(Julia can't watch and turns away.)

VITA: Atta girl, you're doing fine . . .

MABEL: Mary made the most heavenly shepherd's pie in the old days. I lived in that kitchen!

(Mabel inches toward the dining room, recalling a summer day more than seventy years earlier.)

SCENE 4

*The sprawling kitchen in the Tidings's summer house. The
year is 1922. It's mid-July, around two in the afternoon. Mary
O'Neill, the Irish cook, is grinding chunks of cooked lamb in the
meat grinder. She's in her mid-forties and wears a billowing
white apron. Pru, her daughter, eighteen, is mashing potatoes.
Mabel, fifteen, sits at Mary's feet shelling peas. She's at that
awkward stage, wearing a fussy dress that doesn't fit right.*

MABEL: And . . . ?
MARY: He tipped his hat, walked out the door and was
    never seen again.
MABEL: No!
PRU: Good riddance to bad rubbish.
MARY: My only sister. Seduced and abandoned at sixteen.
    (Lowering her voice meaningfully) A year older than
    you.
MABEL: I'd die!
MARY: She almost did, poor thing.
PRU: Look on the bright side, Bridget wouldn't be here if it
    hadn't been for him.
MARY: He wed forty-three times before the constable finally
    caught up with him. Bridget has more half brothers
    and sisters than the daughter of an Arab sheik!
MARY AND PRU *(Chanting)*:
    "Patrick McCann, Patrick McCann,
    forty-three rings on forty-three hands."

MABEL: Awful, awful!

MARY: I don't want you blabbing this all over town, now. My niece Bridget is a good girl. The Lowells are very happy with her.

MABEL: I won't say a word, I promise. Cross my heart and hope to die.

MARY: It's just between us. Our secret

MABEL: My lips are sealed.

PRU *(To Mary)*: Too bad your sister's weren't back when it counted.

MARY *(Swatting her with a towel)*: Prudence Patricia O'Neill!

PRU *(Trying to defend herself)*: Help . . . help!

(They tussle with each other, laughing and squealing.)

MABEL *(To Mary)*: How long have you been married to Norton?

MARY: Let me see . . .

PRU: Well, I'm eighteen.

MARY: It's eighteen years, then.

PRU: Just under the wire.

MABEL: Mama says Norton is the best chauffeur we've ever had.

MARY: Any fool can drive a car.

MABEL: I can't.

(She eats a handful of raw peas.)

PRU: You could if someone taught you how. I've driven a train.

MARY: She's driven a train, she says.

PRU: Well, I have!

MARY: And I've walked on water. How are those potatoes coming?

PRU *(Bearing them aloft)*: Done!

MARY: And when, pray tell, did you drive this train?

PRU: Last week.

MARY: Last week, she says.

PRU: From Revere to Boston.

MARY: From Revere to Boston, is it? *(Handing her a bowl of apples)* Well, I hope you're not too above us all to peel these apples.

(Mabel eats more peas.)

PRU: Buddy let me take the controls.

MARY: That good for nothing! I thought I told you I don't want you seeing him.

PRU: He's a good man, a sweet man, he gives me my way. *(She mimics blasting a train whistle)*

MARY: Men! They're either devils or fools.

PRU *(Peeling an apple)*: Better marry a fool than share a devil with forty-two wives.

(Mabel eats more peas.)

MARY: There, the lamb's ground. I've never seen a family with such a craving for shepherd's pie, to say nothing of its passion for entertaining. Fifteen for dinner every night. Not that I'm complaining, mind you, a full house is a happy house. *(Swatting Mabel with the dish towel)* Stop eating those peas, child! There'll be none left for your guests.

MABEL: I love them raw.

MARY: What will your mother say when Pru passes her an empty vegetable dish?

PRU *(As Maud)*: "Plus ça change, plus c'est la même chose!"

MARY: It's bad enough you spend so much time down here.

MABEL: But I like being with you. It's so much more fun than upstairs.

PRU: I'd trade places in a minute.

MARY: Where did this uppity girl come from?

PRU: The fairies brought me, I was switched at birth.

MARY: You mean, the devil brought you, you're no daughter of mine. Hurry along now, those apples aren't going to peel themselves.

MABEL: I'll do them!

MARY: That's all we need. For you to eat half the dessert as well!

PRU: Look at my hands! *(Thrusting them out)* They're covered with moss.

MARY: That's not moss. It's the freckled skin of a lazy girl.

PRU: I can breathe under water and cast spells.

MARY: It's girls like you that give the Irish a bad name.

PRU *(Incanting over Mabel)*:
"River run, moonbeam glow,
Ask me what you want to know.
Love, adventure, riches, fame,
A glance at your palm,
And I'll see it plain."

MAUD *(Calling from offstage)*: MABEL . . . MABEL . . . NORTON'S WAITING.

MARY: Run along, your mother's calling.

PRU *(Picking up Mabel's hand)*:
"Eye of sheep, lip of hare,
All my prophesies I will share."

MAUD: PHINNEY'S MATCH STARTS IN FORTY-FIVE MINUTES!

MARY: Go on, do as she says.

MABEL: But I want to stay here. *(To Maud)* GO WITHOUT ME.

MARY *(Swatting the towel at her)*: Go, go . . .

MAUD: IT'S THE CHAMPIONSHIP GAME. ALL OF ESSEX COUNTY WILL BE THERE!

MABEL: I'M SICK OF POLO!

MARY *(To Pru)*: Do you believe this girl?

MAUD: GUS . . . MABEL SAYS SHE ISN'T COMING.

PRU *(Examining Mabel's palm)*: Look at this love line . . .

MABEL: What does it say, what does it say?

GUS *(Striding into the kitchen, furious)*: *What's this I hear about you're not coming to Phinney's match?*

(Gus is dressed in fabulous polo-watching attire. Everyone snaps to attention.)

GUS *(Oozing charm)*: Good afternoon, Mary, good afternoon, Pru . . .

MARY: Good afternoon, Mr. Tidings.

PRU *(Curtsying)*: Mr. Tidings.

GUS: Are you both well?

MARY: Very well, thank you.

GUS: Forgive my sudden entrance, but Mrs. Tidings just informed me Mabel doesn't want to go to Phinney's match.

(Maud materializes at his side, looking equally stylish.)

MAUD: She says she's sick of polo . . . Good afternoon Mary, Pru . . .

MARY: Good day, Mrs. Tidings.

PRU *(Curtsying)*: Mrs. Tidings.

MAUD: Are you both well?

MARY: Very well, thank you.

(Frazier bounds into the room. He's now twenty-one and a natty dresser.)

FRAZIER: Porter Bigelow will be there!

MAUD: I can't stand that boy, he drinks too much!

FRAZIER: But he sure is handsome, isn't he Mabel?

MAUD: The whole family drinks too much.

FRAZIER: But Mabel doesn't mind because she's got a crush on him.

MABEL: I do not.

FRAZIER: Do so.

MABEL: Do not!

FRAZIER: Mabel, Mabel, your blushes give you away.
    (He bows to Mary and Pru, doffing an imaginary hat) Mary, Pru . . . sorceresses of the kitchen, purveyors of gastronomic delights, I salute you.

MARY *(Trying not to laugh)*: Master Tidings . . .

(Pru is overcome with the giggles.)

FRAZIER: What are you preparing for tonight's repast?
MARY: Shepherd's pie, sir.
FRAZIER: *Good choice!*
GUS: The *only* choice as far as I'm concerned.
MAUD *(To Mary)*: I hope Mabel isn't getting in your way.
MARY: Not at all, ma'am, we enjoy her company.
GUS: Time's a wasting. Mabel? *(Offering her his arm)*
MABEL: I don't feel well, Papa.
MAUD: Darling . . .
MABEL: I think I'm coming down with something.
FRAZIER: Porter will be heartbroken.

(Mabel starts coughing.)

MAUD: It's the dampness in the air. I've had a headache all
summer.
GUS: Alright, alright, you can stay home.
FRAZIER: Ohh to be a woman.
GUS AND MAUD: *Frazier!*
FRAZIER: I've never cared for polo. Parlor games are more
to my taste.
GUS: Who *is* this boy?
FRAZIER: Your black sheep. *(He baas)*
GUS *(Taking Maud's arm)*: Come along Maud, we don't
want to miss the match.

*(Frazier emits a cavalcade of baas. Mary and Pru
exchange amused glances.)*

GUS: Alright, Frazier . . .
MAUD: That will do.

(A brief silence. Frazier emits a poignant baa.)

GUS *(With blood is his voice)*: ENOUGH IS ENOUGH!

FRAZIER: Easy for you to say.

GUS (*Pulling Maud toward the door*): Maud . . .

MAUD: I'm coming, I'm coming. Now Mabel, I don't want you getting in Mary's hair.

GUS (*Exiting*): And keep an eye on Freddy. The croquet party's Saturday. I want that lawn as smooth as glass. Remember what happened to Chandler Coffin last summer. He sprained his ankle on a tuft of weeds.

MAUD: Well, what do you expect? It's amazing the boy can play at all, given that pathetic club foot of his.

MABEL (*Stung*): Mama! . . .

(*Norton beeps the horn.*)

GUS: Norton's honking, we've got to go.

FRAZIER (*Exiting*): If I see Porter, I'll give him a kiss for you. (*He emits a final baa*)

MAUD (*Halfway down the hall*): I'm just as glad she's not coming, she's so moody these days.

(*Doors slam, the car starts up and drives away. Silence.*)

MABEL: Well . . .

PRU: So . . .

(*The silence deepens.*)

MARY (*Surveying the room*): What am I forgetting?

MABEL (*Pulling at her bodice*): I've got to get out of this dress, I can't breathe.

MARY: *The brandy sauce!* Come on, Pru, help me!

PRU (*To Mabel*): See what I have to put up with? I'm not only the serving girl, I'm also her slave.

MARY: I gave you life and don't you forget it!

MABEL (*Heading toward the door*): I'm going to change into my bathing suit.

MARY: I should have known it was a plot to go swimming. I've never seen anyone spend so much time in the water. What on earth do you think about, hour after hour?

MABEL: Nothing, really. I count my strokes and sing songs.

MARY *(Working on the brandy sauce)*: Songs? What kind of songs?

MABEL: Nursery rhymes, mostly. "Row, Row, Row Your Boat," "The Farmer in the Dell." I sing each one two hundred times and then move on to another.

PRU: I'd go mad.

MABEL: It's relaxing, actually.

MARY: The girl is daft. She paddles through the freezing ocean, singing nursery rhymes. *(She starts singing)*
"Row, row, row your boat,
Gently down the stream . . ."

MARY:	PRU:
"Merrily, merrily, merrily, merrily, Life is but a dream."	"Row, row, row your boat, Gently down the stream. Merrily, merrily, merrily, merrily, Life is but a dream."

(Silence.)

MABEL: I'd swim around the world if I could.

PRU: What if a whale comes along?

MABEL: They're miles away, out in the open sea.

PRU: Or an octopus?

MARY *(Waving her arms, taunting Pru)*: Or a squid!

PRU *(Squirming)*: Uuugh, stop!

MARY *(Making lurid gestures)*: Or the Loch Ness Monster!

PRU: No, no!

MARY: My mother saw Nessie on her tenth birthday. She said it was the size of Buckingham Palace. *(More menacing gestures)*

PRU *(Shrinking from Mary)*: Noooo!

MARY (*Rushing at Pru like the Loch Ness Monster*): I'm going to get you . . .

PRU (*Throwing her arms around Mabel in a panic*): SAVE ME, SAVE ME . . .

MARY (*Putting on a Scottish accent as she chases them*): Dinna think you can get away from *me*, me lassies . . . Lunch, lunch . . . it's time for me lunch!

MABEL AND PRU: HELP, HELP, HELP, HELLLLLLLLP!

(*The chase becomes more frantic as Mabel and Pru shriek in terror. Mary finally catches them and they fall into a squealing heap.*)

PRU: Stop, stop, I'm going to wet my knickers!

MABEL: Help, murder police . . .

MARY (*Back to herself*): There, there, I'd never hurt my precious girls.

(*They gradually calm down. Mary pats their cheeks and straightens their hair.*)

MARY: You're going to be the death of me with your foolish games.

PRU: *Our* foolish games? *You* were the one that started it.

MABEL (*Pulling away*): I've got to get going, I only have a few hours.

MARY: Be careful now, don't tire yourself out.

MABEL: Don't forget to wave when I go past.

MARY: Do we ever?

MABEL: It keeps me going.

PRU: You should see yourself. You're no bigger than a pea, bobbing up and down.

MARY: On to China, then.

MABEL: On to China!

(*She pauses a moment before dashing out of the room. Mary and Pru gaze after her as the lights slowly dim.*)

SCENE 5

The present. Later that afternoon. Mabel's sitting in her dark-ened bedroom by the phone. She's going over the guest list for her party. A light rain falls. The foghorn moans in the distance.

M A B E L : Chandler, Kitty Lowell, Isobel Sargent, Gabby Ames and the doddering Wheelocks, if they're still alive. Damned guest list . . . I'd better get a wiggle on before they all drop dead. *(Flipping through her address book)* Lowell, Lowell . . . here we go . . . 822-0551 . . . *(She dials, waits and then speaks very loud)* KITTY, IT'S M. T. JULIA'S IN TOWN. SHE JUST GOT IN FROM PARIS, IF YOU PLEASE, SO I'M PLANNING A LITTLE CROQUET PARTY OVER THE FOURTH AND WAS HOPING YOU COULD COME. I FOUND SOME OF GRANDMOTHER'S HEAVENLY OLD LAWN DRESSES SO WE CAN REALLY LOOK LIKE SOME-THING . . . *(Listening)* HMMMM? I CAN'T HEAR YOU, YOU'LL HAVE TO SPEAK UP. *(Listening)* WHAT'S THAT? OH, I'M SORRY, I MUST HAVE DIALED THE WRONG NUMBER. *(She hangs up)* How embarrassing! I'd better look this up again. *(Flipping through her address book)* Lowell, Lowell . . . 822-0557. That sounds more like it. *(Reciting as she dials)* 822-0557 . . . KITTY, JULIA'S IN TOWN, SO I'M GIVING A LITTLE CROQUET PARTY OVER THE FOURTH. Oh no, it's one of those dreadful answering machines. God, I hate those things! *(Listening)* Why do they always have to play music? *(Singing along)* "And in foggy London town the sun is shining . . ." *(Then giving her message very fast)* I'M GIVING A CROQUET PARTY ON THE FOURTH OF JULY, GOOD-BYE! *(She hangs up)* Well done, if I do say so myself. *(Pause)* Oh no, I think I forgot to say who I was, I'll have to call back . . . *(The phone suddenly rings. Mabel jumps and then picks up the receiver)* HELLO? *(Listening)* WELL, *FINALLY!* I'VE BEEN TRYING TO REACH YOU FOR HOURS! . . . WHAT'S THAT? *(Listening)* MRS. McCLOUD FROM THE VISITING NURSE SERVICE? I THOUGHT YOU WERE KITTY LOWELL. *(Listening)* MY BREASTS ARE ON YOUR LAP? . . . *(Listening)* *MY TESTS CAME BACK FROM THE LAB!* WHAT TESTS? *(Listening)* OH YES, MY BLOOD TESTS, I REMEMBER THOSE . . . SLOW DOWN, SLOW DOWN . . . *(Listening)* THE DOCTOR'S CONCERNED? HE WANTS TO SEE ME AGAIN? TOO MANY BRIGHT FLOOD SWELLS? *(Listening) WHITE BLOOD CELLS!* *(Listening)* THERE'S AN UPROAR IN THE FIRMAMENT? YOU'LL HAVE TO CALL BACK WHEN VITA'S HERE, I CAN'T UNDERSTAND A WORD YOU'RE SAYING! *(She slams the receiver down, but misses the cradle)* Damn phone! Go where you belong! *(Slamming it again and again)* Nothing ever works when you want it to! *(She finally hits the cradle)* That's more like it! *(Pause. She sighs and looks around)* Where was I? Oh yes, my guest list . . . I don't remember giving parties being this strenuous . . . *(Gazing around the room)* God, it's dark in here, no wonder I can't see anything. Damn lamp! Why is Vita always moving you? I've told her I want you next to my chair, not halfway across the room! *(She gropes for it, just missing)* Uuuugh . . . ugggh! *(She lunges for it and it falls with a crash)* HELP, I JUST KNOCKED OVER THE LAMP! HELP! HELLLP! . . . *(Pause)* HELLLLOOOO? . . . ANYBODY

HOME? Where is everybody? VIIIIIITAAAAA? *(Silence)*
I must have sent her to the market. *(Pause)* JULIA, OH
JUUUULIAAAA? That's right, she and Minty wanted
to swim in the rain. I'm on my own for a couple of hours.
Nothing wrong with that, I could use a little peace and
quiet for a change. I just can't see anything . . . I can't
walk, I can't hear, my white blood cells are all out of
whack . . . We all know what *that* means. Good old
cancer. No fun, that. No fun at all. It got both Porter
and David Bloom. Dead at fifty-one. Who would have
thought . . . ? God, I miss him! Those hands, that voice,
the kisses . . . *(She starts to break down)* Stop it, Mabel,
stop it right this minute! *(She begins to sing:)*
"Row, row, row your boat,
Gently down the stream . . ."

(West suddenly enters.)

WEST: Anybody home?
MABEL *(Startled)*: Who's that?
WEST: MOM?
MABEL: *David?*
WEST: Mrs. B.?
MABEL: West?
WEST: Are you alright?
MABEL: Where am I?
WEST: In your bedroom.
MABEL: I thought I heard gulls.
WEST: What happened to the lamp?
MABEL: What lamp?
WEST: There's glass all over the floor.
MABEL *(Taking deep gulps of air)*: God, God, God . . .
WEST *(Walking over to her)*: Are you OK?
MABEL: For a minute there I thought you were . . .
WEST: I'm sorry, I didn't mean to scare you.
MABEL: I have to catch my breath.

WEST: Can I get you anything?

MABEL: Would you be kind enough to hand me that shawl. I'm freezing.

WEST *(Picking up a Victorian, fringed shawl)*: This?

MABEL: Please.

WEST *(Handing it to her)*: Here you go.

MABEL: Thank you, West, you're a true gentleman.

WEST: That's a first!

MABEL *(Unfurling it)*: God, this brings back memories! *(Whirling it around her)* "Blow winds and crack your cheeks! Rage . . . !" *(She sends a bunch of knickknacks flying)* Take that you stupid doctors with your tests . . .

WEST: Go, Mrs.B.!

MABEL: I never saw such goings on!

WEST: You show 'em!

MABEL: Barium enemas and CAT scans . . . *(More knick-knacks fly)*

WEST: Yes!

MABEL: Abdominal probes and ash cans. *(And more knick-knacks)*

WEST: Do it!

MABEL: Exploratory surgery and handstands! *I can't take it anymore! (Flinging the shawl to the floor)*

WEST: Easy, easy . . .

MABEL *(Trying to rise, seeing a sudden hallucination)*: The horses are loose . . . They bare their teeth and rush headlong into the sea . . .

WEST: *(At her side)*: Easy, easy . . .

MABEL: Look out, look out, they're coming this way!

WEST: Mrs B.?

MABEL *(Clutching onto him)*: Hold me, David! Hold me! Hold me! Hold me!

(West attempts to comfort her as the lights fade. They rise on Anton Gurevitch tossing the same shawl in a spirited game of charades many years earlier. We hear the sound of breaking china in the background.)

SCENE 6

*A balmy August evening in 1927. The Tidingses are in the
midst of a game of charades in the drawing room with Anton
Gurevitch, mid-forties, the charismatic Russian conductor of
the Boston Symphony Orchestra. Maud, Phinney and
Gurevitch are playing against Chandler, Frazier and Mabel.
Everyone's dressed to the nines. Gurevitch whirls the shawl.
There's the sound of breaking china.*

GUREVITCH: "Blow, winds, and crack your cheeks! . . .
  Rage!"

PHINNEY: Good-bye demitasse cups!

CHANDLER: Don't *say* it, Maestro.

MAUD *(Laughing)*: If only the patrons of the Boston
  Symphony Orchestra could see you now . . .

CHANDLER: You're supposed to act it out!

MAUD: The great Anton Gurevitch lunging like a bull in a
  china shop!

CHANDLER: Stop the game.

GUREVITCH: "Blow you cataracts and hurrianoes, spout
  till you have drencht our steeples . . ."

CHANDLER: He gave it away.

GUREVITCH: I like this charades.

CHANDLER *(Calling offstage)*: M. T . . . FRAZIER . . . THE
  MAESTRO JUST GAVE IT AWAY.

MAUD: And no props, Gurey. It's against the rules.

GUREVITCH: "Props?"

MAUD: That shawl.

GUREVITCH: I use it to make picture.

MAUD, CHANDLER AND PHINNEY: But it's not allowed!

GUREVITCH *(Whirling the shawl)*: You see great king lost in madness.

PHINNEY: Let's hear it for the lunatics!

MAUD: And you're not supposed to *speak*!

GUREVITCH: A tempest howls in his breaking heart.

(Frazier enters dressed in an Edwardian morning coat. He grabs the shawl from Gurevitch.)

FRAZIER: I'd hate to be around when he conducts the *1812 Overture.*

GUREVITCH: First word . . . *(He mimics blowing)*

CHANDLER: You already told them.

MAUD AND PHINNEY: "Blow!"

CHANDLER *(To Frazier)*: He recited the entire thing!

GUREVITCH: Second word . . . *(He mimics being the wind)*

CHANDLER: I'm not playing anymore.

MAUD AND PHINNEY: "Wind."

CHANDLER: This isn't fair.

GUREVITCH: Fourth word. *(He mimics crack)*

MAUD AND PHINNEY: "Blow winds and crack your cheeks! Rage!"

(Mabel enters carrying glasses of champagne. She's twenty and has blossomed into a beauty. Both Chandler and Gurevitch are smitten with her. Gurevitch stops playing and rushes to her side.)

GUREVITCH: There you are!

CHANDLER:
". . . Fairer than the evening air,
Clad in the beauty of a thousand stars."

MABEL: Please!

FRAZIER: What about *me*? *(Draping the shawl around himself)* "Mirror, mirror, on the wall, who's the fairest of

them all?" *(Answering as the mirror)* "Why you, oh
queen! Snow White is just a child!"

MAUD *(Linking arms with Gurevitch)*: Thank God Gus is off
on one of his sails, he'd be appalled at our goings-on.

MABEL: Poor Papa.

PHINNEY: On the contrary, he knows where he belongs.

FRAZIER: *Not* here!

MAUD: If only he weren't alone.

FRAZIER: No one wants to go with him, given his temper.

MAUD: I worry so.

FRAZIER: He'll be alright. Only the good die young.

MAUD AND MABEL: *Frazier!*

PHINNEY: If they're lucky!

MABEL: Phinney!

MAUD: Doesn't he realize he's tempting fate?

PHINNEY: That's the whole point. To risk it all.

MAUD: But why New Zealand?

PHINNEY: One perfect dive . . . and then oblivion.

CHANDLER: "Between extremities Man runs his course."

FRAZIER *(Unwinding the cape and trailing it on the floor)*: I,
on the other hand, prefer to stay home with the ladies.

GUREVITCH: Every course has its perils.

FRAZIER: Indeed it does, Maestro, indeed it does.

(Silence.)

MAUD: Enough of this gloom, on with the game!

ALL: On with the game!

MABEL: Where were we?

MAUD: It's your turn to act out *our* charade, and I've come
up with a killer, a *killer*! *(She writes it down and shows
it to Gurevitch and Phinney with sadistic glee)*

PHINNEY: Good God!

GUREVITCH: "Jabberwocky?" This is not English!

MAUD *(In a stage whisper)*: *Au contraire!* Lewis Carroll is
the most English of Englishmen. *Alice in Wonderland*
is a classic!

GUREVITCH: What is this "slithy toves?"

MAUD: Shhh, not so loud!

PHINNEY: It can't be done.

MAUD *(Handing it to Mabel)*: Alright, my pretty, try *this* on for size!

MABEL *(Reads it aghast)*: Mama!

(Maud rubs her hands and cackles like a wicked step-mother.)

MABEL: You're right, it's impossible.

MAUD: That's the whole point!

MABEL *(Reading it in a stage whisper to herself)*:
"Twas brillig, and the slithy toves
Did gyre and gimble in the wabe . . ."

MAUD: This is *my* game!

MABEL: Where do I begin?

MAUD *(Pulling out a stopwatch)*: On your mark . . .

MABEL *(Clasping her hands)*:
"Our Father who art in heaven,
Hallowed be thy name . . ."

MAUD: Get set . . .

MABEL:
"Thy kingdom come,
Thy will be . . ."

MAUD: GO!

(Chandler and Frazier take their places. Mabel indicates it's from a poem.)

CHANDLER AND FRAZIER: A poem!

(Mabel indicates it's thirteen words.)

CHANDLER AND FRAZIER: Thirteen words!

(Mabel indicates the first word.)

CHANDLER AND FRAZIER: First word . . .
MABEL *(In a stage whisper)*: "Twas . . ." *(She pulls her ear)*
CHANDLER AND FRAZIER: Sounds like . . .

(Mabel mimics an insect.)

CHANDLER: Bee!
FRAZIER: Hornet!
CHANDLER: Mosquito!

(Mabel mimics an insect more intensely.)

CHANDLER: Buzz!

(Mabel excitedly nods yes, pulling her ear.)

CHANDLER AND FRAZIER: Sounds like buzz!
CHANDLER: Does!
FRAZIER: Cuz!
CHANDLER: Fuzz!
FRAZIER: Was!
CHANDLER: "Fuzzy wuzzy, was a bear . . ."
FRAZIER: "Fuzzy, wuzzy had no hair . . ."
CHANDLER: "Fuzzy wuzzy, wasn't fuzzy . . ."
FRAZIER: "Was he?"
MAUD: One minute and forty-five seconds to go . . .

(Mabel indicates word number five.)

CHANDLER AND FRAZIER: Fifth word.

(Mabel pulls on her ear.)

CHANDLER AND FRAZIER: Sounds like . . .
MABEL *(In a stage whisper)*: "Slithy."

(She goes into contortions trying to be slimy.)

MAUD (*Leaning into Gurevitch, awash with laughter*): Poor thing. It's hopeless, *hopeless!*

CHANDLER: Sticky!

FRAZIER: Gooey!

CHANDLER: Greasy!

(Mabel acts slimier.)

FRAZIER: Slippery!

CHANDLER: Slimy!

(Mabel nods yes, and pulls on her ear, wild with excitement.)

CHANDLER AND FRAZIER: Sounds like *slimy!*

CHANDLER: Blimy!

FRAZIER: Stymie!

CHANDLER: Tie me up and throw me down!

(Mabel nods no and indicates the sixth word.)

CHANDLER AND FRAZIER: Word number six.

MABEL (*In a stage whisper*): "Toves." *(She pulls her ear)*

CHANDLER AND FRAZIER: Sounds like . . .

(Mabel imitates a toad.)

FRAZIER: Frog!

GUREVITCH: *Toad!*

(Mabel nods yes.)

MAUD (*Cuffing Gurevitch*): Maestro, you're not on their side!

GUREVITCH (*Hanging his head*): Sorry, sorry . . .

(Mabel indicates words five and six, pulling her ear.)

CHANDLER: Sounds like *slimy toads* . . .

(Mabel nods yes and does more toadlike moves.)

FRAZIER:
"Squat like a toad,
Close at the ear of Eve . . ."

(Mabel nods no.)

CHANDLER: "I had rather be a toad and live upon the vapor of a dungeon than keep a corner in the thing I love . . ."

(Mabel nods no.)

FRAZIER *(As Richard III)*:
"A toad, a toad!
My kingdom for a toad!"
MAUD: One minute left!

(Mabel indicates words eight and ten.)

CHANDLER AND FRAZIER: Words eight and ten.
MABEL *(In a stage whisper)*: "Gyre and gimble." *(She pulls her ear)*
CHANDLER AND FRAZIER: Sounds like . . .

(Mabel launches into an extraordinary dance, part gyration and part nimble soft-shoe.)

CHANDLER: Saint Vitas dance!
FRAZIER *(Singing)*: Charleston, Charleston . . .
CHANDLER: The Gypsy King Rag!
FRAZIER: Hootchie-Kootchie!
CHANDLER: Hotsie-Totsie!
GUREVITCH: The Siberian Two-Step! *(He rises, grabs Mabel and launches into a spirited folk dance, singing snatches of Russian)*

MAUD: Gurey, Gurey, you're not on their side!

(Chandler and Frazier start clapping in time.)

CHANDLER: The Moscow Mazurka!
FRAZIER: The Petrograd Polka!
PHINNEY: The Bolshevik Backflip! The Russians are excellent divers, you know.
MAUD *(With blood in her voice)*: Thirty-four seconds!

(Mabel pulls away from Gurevitch and indicates that she's going to act out the entire poem.)

CHANDLER AND FRAZIER: The whole idea!
PHINNEY: That's my sister!

(Mabel takes a deep breath and launches into a fantastic rendering of "Jabberwocky," complete with gyrations, soft-shoe and tap. It gets increasingly lurid and violent as everyone watches, open-mouthed.)

CHANDLER:
"Twas brillig, and the slithy toves
Did gyre and gimble in the wabe."
MABEL *(Throwing herself at him)*: Yes, yes!
FRAZIER *(Dancing around them)*: "Jabberwocky" from *Alice in Wonderland*!
MABEL: We did it, we did it!
CHANDLER *(Covering her with kisses)*: You were brilliant *brilliant*!
PHINNEY *(Applauding Mabel)*: Bravo, M. T.! Neatly done!
MAUD: Just one minute. How did you figure that out, Chan?
CHANDLER: Intuition.
MAUD: But you didn't get one word!
CHANDLER: I know what she's thinking.
MAUD: Not one!
CHANDLER: You know, two hearts that beat as one and all that.

MAUD: Well, what do you expect? His father is Titus Coffin, one of the great poets of our time. He wrote the most beautiful poem about the high-dive after Phinney won his Olympic medal. How did it go?

PHINNEY *(Covering his ears)*: Mama, *please . . .*

MAUD: It was a paraphrase of Swinburne.

PHINNEY: You're embarrassing me!

FRAZIER: No one wrote a poem after I joined Papa's firm.

CHANDLER:

> "Shot like a stone from a sling through the air,
> Shouting and laughing with delight,
> He plunged head foremost into the approaching wave."

FRAZIER: But then again, I've hardly distinguished myself as a great legal mind.

PHINNEY: Now, now . . .

FRAZIER: Good old Frazier Tidings. Born with a silver shovel in his mouth. Privilege isn't all it's cracked up to be.

MABEL: More, more, let's play another round!

MAUD *(Resting her head on Gurevitch's shoulder)*: You seem to forget, Maestro Gurevitch has to sail for Vienna tomorrow, he's a very busy man. He conducts all over the world.

MABEL: Please, please? Pretty please? Just one more round?

MAUD: I don't know where you find the time to join us in our silly parlor games.

GUREVITCH *(Drifting away from Maud and putting his arm around Mabel)*: You know us Russians, we have a weakness for beautiful women.

MABEL: Maestro!

GUREVITCH *(Drawing her close)*: As our literature so tragically attests.

(A brief silence. The grandfather clock starts to strike eleven.)

CHANDLER *(Improvising)*:

> "And so the hours of the clock parade,
> As we stand poised for our next charade . . ."

MAUD: Just like his father. It's in the blood.

CHANDLER:
"The maestro swoons, hearing music of the spheres,
While we poor fools depend on our ears.
Tis ever thus with games and art,
The great ones inhabit a world apart."

(Chandler bows, doffing an imaginary hat. Gurevitch returns the bow. Chandler executes a more florid one. Gurevitch tops him. Everyone laughs.)

GUREVITCH: Where did you find this extraordinary young man?

MAUD: He's been a friend of the family for years. Groton, Harvard, swimming . . .

CHANDLER *(Exaggerating his limp)*: I, however, lack Phinney's grace, as you may have noticed.

PHINNEY: I merely enter the water, you travel through it.

MABEL: Last year he swam the Hellespont.

CHANDLER: Like that other famous clubfoot, Lord Byron!

MAUD, PHINNEY, FRAZIER AND MABEL: *Chandler!*

CHANDLER: Come, come, it makes life so much easier if you call a spade a spade, deformed as it may be. I come from a noble, if somewhat shady line starting with Oedipus. Fortunately there's not much chance I'll follow in his footsteps—pardon the pun—since my distinguished father is very much alive and gives every indication of living forever. Long live the king!

MABEL: I just got a great idea! In honor of it's being the end of summer, how about a swim to Singing Beach!

MAUD: Now?

FRAZIER: TO SINGING BEACH!

CHANDLER: "Roll on thou deep and dark blue ocean, roll . . ."

MAUD: But it's pitch-black outside.

MABEL: On the contrary!

(She rushes to a window and pulls back the curtains. A stream of moonlight floods the room. Everyone gasps.)

GUREVITCH: Look at that moon . . .

MAUD: The girl has eyes in the back of her head!

GUREVITCH (*Putting an arm around Mabel*): And such lovely eyes.

CHANDLER: ". . . those silent tongues of love."

MAUD (*Pulling Mabel away from Gurevitch*): Yes, our little Mabel has developed into quite a beauty. It's a pity she has such appalling taste in men.

MABEL: Mama!

MAUD: She only cares for that wretched Porter Bigelow.

FRAZIER: I like him.

PHINNEY: He's a good man.

MAUD: But he drinks like a fish.

FRAZIER: Porter's got style.

PHINNEY: And a great throwing arm.

FRAZIER: He marches to his own drummer. (*Banging an imaginary drum*) Ba-boom, ba-boom . . .

PHINNEY: He was the greatest quarterback Harvard ever had! (*Mimes throwing a pretend pass to Frazier*)

MAUD: I've never seen that boy sober. But then I've never seen *any* of the Bigelows sober.

FRAZIER (*Mimes catching the pass*): Ba-boom!

MABEL: He just got a seat on the stock exchange.

MAUD: Well, let's hope he doesn't fall out of it!

(*Phinney and Frazier mime their game in slow motion.*)

MABEL (*Covering her ears*): I don't have to listen to this.

MAUD: As my mother used to say, "Stay away from handsome men, you'll always be fighting over the mirror."

FRAZIER: Easier said than done.

CHANDLER: Tell that to the girls.

PHINNEY (*Throwing another pass*): Porter's the most sought-after bachelor in Boston.

CHANDLER: In Massachusetts!

FRAZIER (*Catching it*): Ba-boom!

MAUD: You should have seen his father in his day. Quincy Bigelow was blinding, *blinding*!

CHANDLER: Ahh, beauty . . .

FRAZIER: The great destroyer . . .

CHANDLER: "Ever ancient and ever new."

(Silence.)

GUREVITCH: Now about this swim . . .

MABEL, PHINNEY, FRAZIER AND CHANDLER: TO SINGING BEACH!

GUREVITCH: Singing Beach?

MAUD: It's the public beach in Manchester. I don't approve at all.

CHANDLER: How about you, Maestro, do you swim?

GUREVITCH: Do I swim? I grew up in Odessa on the Black Sea.

MABEL: You can borrow one of Papa's bathing suits.

CHANDLER: You don't have to worry about me, since I always swim in the nude.

MAUD AND MABEL: *Chandler?!*

CHANDLER: Only kidding, only kidding . . .

MAUD: It's one thing staying up half the night playing charades, but swimming to Singing Beach? What would your father say?

ALL BUT MAUD: *He isn't here!*

GUREVITCH: While the cat's away, the mice will play! *(He pinches Mabel's bottom)*

MAUD: Gurey!

MABEL: To Singing Beach!

MAUD: Hold your horses . . .

MABEL *(Heading for the door)*: Last one out's a rotten egg!

MAUD *(Blocking her way)*: You're not leaving this house!

MABEL: *Mama?!*

MAUD: It's bad enough the Tidings *men* go traipsing all over kingdom come . . .

PHINNEY: I'll keep an eye on her.

CHANDLER (*Putting his arm around her*): Me too.

GUREVITCH (*Putting his arm around her*): We'll *all* keep an eye on her.

(*They gaze at Mabel adoringly.*)

PHINNEY: If we can keep up.

CHANDLER: She's faster than all of us.

PHINNEY: It's embarrassing.

CHANDLER: Humiliating.

MABEL: And about time!

MAUD: Well, you're not going and that's that!

MABEL: Why not?

MAUD: Because young ladies don't go swimming in the middle of the night!

MABEL: What about Gertrude Ederle?

MAUD: Gertrude Ederle? Who on earth is she?

MABEL: The "young lady" who swam the English Channel last year.

MAUD: "Ederle?" What kind of name is that?

MABEL: Setting a new world record, if you please.

MAUD: It sounds German.

MABEL: Fourteen hours and thirty-nine minutes.

CHANDLER: She's from New York. Her father's a butcher.

MAUD: A *butcher*? What next?

MABEL: Of course she did it from France to England which is the easier route. A woman has yet to do it from England to France.

CHANDLER: And only nineteen!

MABEL: *A year younger than I!*

CHANDLER: I met her once. Nice girl. Strong as an ox.

FRAZIER (*Shuddering*): I can imagine.

MAUD: Well, what do you expect coming from *that* background? (*To Mabel*) You, on the other hand, are delicate.

MABEL: *Delicate?*

MAUD: You've got a spot on your lung.

MABEL: Everyone in Boston has a spot on their lung!

FRAZIER: I have four!

PHINNEY *(Cuffing him)*: You!

(They scuffle.)

CHANDLER:
"Glory be to God for *dappled* things—
For skies of couple-color as a brinded cow;
For rose-moles all in stipple upon trout that swim."

MABEL: I happen to have the endurance of a horse. I'll let you in on a secret. I'm in training to swim the Channel from England to France.

MAUD: *What did you say?*

MABEL: Last week I swam to Eastern Point.

PHINNEY AND FRAZIER: Eastern Point?

MAUD: *That's beyond Rockport!*

PHINNEY: I'm impressed.

FRAZIER *(Heading out the door)*: I'm leaving!

MAUD: I won't stand for it!

FRAZIER: My brother an Olympic diver, my sister a Channel swimmer . . .

MABEL *(Pulling him back in)*: Fray . . .

FRAZIER: I'm going outside to slit my wrists.

CHANDLER: You should have seen her.

MAUD *(Covering her ears)*: I don't want to hear. Ba, ba, ba, ba . . .

FRAZIER: Me either. Ba, ba, ba, ba . . .

CHANDLER: She was magnificent.

MABEL: Chandler's helping me train.

CHANDLER: I was beside her the whole time. That is, when I could keep up.

MAUD: *Are you trying to give me a heart attack?*

CHANDLER: She wasn't even tired.

MAUD: We'll discuss this later.

MABEL: I have sponsors, Mama.

MAUD: *Sponsors?*

MABEL: The Coffins, the Shaws, Reverend Graves . . .

MAUD: Reverend *Graves?* You've talked to Reverend *Graves?*

MABEL: Felicity Beaumont, Tippy Loring, Margaret Rantoul, the Saltonstalls, the Sedgewicks, the strapping Ames sisters . . .

MAUD: Stop, stop . . .

PHINNEY: That's our baby sister!

FRAZIER: Leaving us all in the dust!

MAUD *(Staggering to a chair)*: ENOUGH, I SAY, ENOUGH!

(An awful silence.)

GUREVITCH *(Looking at his watch)*: Well, it's getting late.

MAUD *(Rises, taking Gurevitch's arm)*: It *is* getting late . . . We always have such fun when you come over, I wish we saw more of you, I'm a virtual widow.

FRAZIER: And she loves every minute of it.

GUREVITCH *(Pulling her close)*: Maudie, Maudie . . .

FRAZIER: Look at her, she fairly glows with relief!

MAUD *(To Gurevitch)*: See what fresh children I have to put up with?

MABEL: Not fresh, Mama, and not children anymore.

MAUD: I beg your pardon?

MABEL: I've been preparing this swim for years. Sneaking out of the house at dawn, summer after summer. I passed your window a million times. You heard me, but you were so wrapped up in your own misery, you never raised the blinds to look . . . *(She kicks off her shoes)*

MAUD: What are you talking about?

MABEL: One would think you would have been curious. I could have had a lover at my side or a desperado trying to kidnap me at knife point.

MAUD: I'm not listening to this.

MABEL: You heard me. I tossed gravel at the glass to make sure . . . The servants loved it. *(She rolls down her stockings)*

MAUD: The *servants* saw you?

MABEL: They cheered me on, waving dish towels from their windows.

MAUD (*To Phinney and Frazier*): *Did you know about this?*

MABEL: Of course they knew. Everyone knew. Papa's been watching me for years. He'd open an eye and wink at me. Those winks propelled me all the way to Gloucester and back, but it was *your* gaze I was desperate for. (*She starts unbuttoning her dress*) I kept looking at the window, willing you to lift the shade and finally see me. (*Imitating her*) "Good grief, it's Mabel! Look at her go! Past the Codman's, past the Adams's and Rantoul's!" But no such luck. The shade was always drawn. The disdain . . . no, lack of interest . . . It was really quite extraordinary . . . Your "delicate" daughter, plowing through the Atlantic right under your nose . . .

CHANDLER: Off, off, take it off!

PHINNEY: Go, M. T.!

FRAZIER: Do it for all of us!

MAUD: *See here, young lady* . . .

GUREVITCH: She's magnificent!

CHANDLER:
"Nymph, in thy orisons,
Be all my sins remembered."

MABEL: I could have gotten a cramp and drowned . . . Not that you would have saved me, but at least you could have watched me go down. (*Struggling as if in the water*) "Help . . . helllp . . . helllllp . . ." (*She starts to shimmy out of her dress*)

MAUD: I WON'T HAVE THIS SORT OF BEHAVIOR IN MY HOUSE!

MABEL: But drowning wasn't on my mind. I wanted you to see me swim. I imagined a pattern was involved. "She'll raise the shade after the fiftieth stroke, the seventieth, the hundredth . . ." And back and forth I'd go, swimming parallel to the house for the first hour or so. Then I thought it had to do with speed. "If I go faster, she'll raise it." (*Flinging her dress to the floor*) So I'd do seventy strokes a minute, eighty, ninety, pushing myself to the limit. (*Mabel stands revealed in a bathing suit, 1920s style*) Look at me, Mama, look at me! . . .

GUREVITCH: (*Whistling and applauding*): Brava, brava!

PHINNEY: Nicely done!

FRAZIER: *Brilliant!*

CHANDLER: I'm in love.

MABEL (*In tears*): Look at me!

GUREVITCH: Ah youth . . .

MAUD (*In a towering rage*): THE PARTY'S OVER! GO TO YOUR ROOM!

MABEL (*To herself*): Let it go, Mabel, let it go.

(*Silence as Mabel struggles to control herself.*)

MAUD: YOU HEARD ME!

MABEL (*Singing in a breaking voice*):
"The farmer in the dell,
The farmer in the dell,
Hi-ho the dairy-o,
The farmer in the dell."

MAUD (*Heading for the door*): THAT'S IT! I'M WIRING YOUR FATHER!

MABEL: I can swim for miles. Past islands and continents, into other times zones.

MAUD: YOU'RE NOT LEAVING THIS HOUSE FOR THE REST OF THE SUMMER!

MABEL: You can't forbid me to swim. I've left you behind. You're so far away I can't even see you.

(*Maud storms out of the room. No one moves. Everyone looks at Mabel. She raises her arms and slowly turns toward the ocean as the curtain slowly falls.*)

ACT TWO

SCENE 1

The present. Four days later, it's five o'clock in the morning and still dark. Wearing a tattered nightgown and robe, Mabel is looking for something in the hall closet. The only light comes from a dim bulb inside the closet. She probes through the wilderness of junk with her long pincers while steadying herself on her walker. The foghorn moans in the distance.

MABEL: Where *is* that damned croquet set?

(Something falls with a crash.)

MABEL: Gently, gently . . . I don't want to wake everyone up. *(Pulling out a folding tripod chair)* Mercy, I haven't seen this in ages! It was Mama's. She used to take it to Phinney's polo matches . . . Poor Phin, broke his neck doing a swan dive off the Rock of Gibraltar. Too much fame and too much drink . . . Gone, gone . . . they're all gone. Frazier a suicide at thirty-one, Papa lost off the Cape of Good Hope, Mama a catastrophic stroke in the Public Gardens . . . Face down in the zinnias, kerplop! I'm the only one left, the end of the line, the sediment at the bottom of the glass . . . Who would have thought? *(She sighs)* Oh well, *c'est la guerre!* *(Pulling out a beat-up pair of binoculars)* Papa's binoculars! I don't believe it! *(Surveying the room through them)* Good Lord, when did things start getting so shabby? It looks like Tobacco Road in here! The paint's peeling off the ceiling and the slipcovers are in tatters. *(Making her way over to the chair)* What happened to the painting that used to be in that frame? Don't tell me I sold it? I loved that painting. The broody sky and those precious sheep . . . I must have needed the money . . . *(Sitting down with a thud)* Ugh!

(There's a crash behind the Chinese screen.)

MABEL *(Hand flying to her heart)*: What was that? Is someone there? Hello? Hello?

(Mabel peers into the darkness. The screen starts to move toward her.)

MABEL: If you're a burglar, show yourself and get it over with. I can't stand shilly-shallying around!

(Minty pops her head out from behind the screen.)

MABEL: *Minty!* What are you doing here?
MINTY: I couldn't sleep.
MABEL: Speak up, speak up.
MINTY: *I said, I couldn't sleep!*
MABEL: It's the damned foghorn. God, I hate that thing! *(She moans in tandem with it)* Come and keep me company, I won't bite.

(Minty doesn't move.)

MABEL: I was looking for our old croquet set.

(Silence.)

MABEL: Hello? Are you still there? *(Silence)* Come out so I can see you.

(Minty inches out from behind the screen. She's wearing parts of Vita's Paul Revere costume.)

MABEL: Mercy, it's Paul Revere again!

MINTY: Vita said I could try it on.

MABEL: He's all over the place!

MINTY *(Putting on the hat and striking a pose)*:
"One if by land and two if by sea,
and I on the opposite shore will be!"

MABEL: Bravo! Nicely done!

MINTY: I'm going to be an actress when I grow up.

MABEL: A princess! How grand.

MINTY: Not a princess, an *actress*!

MABEL: An actress?

MINTY: I had the lead in our school play, *Le Petit Prince*.

MABEL: *The Pretty Pants?*

MINTY: *Le Petit Prince, The Little Prince.*

MABEL: *Le Petit Prince!* I used to love that book!

MINTY: It was so much fun. Mommy came both nights.

MABEL: Hmmm?

MINTY: *I said, Mommy came both nights!*

MABEL: Well, Paris is very damp.

MINTY: Daddy didn't see me, though. He's never home.

MABEL: Speak up, speak up!

MINTY: I SAID, DADDY'S NEVER HOME!

MABEL *(Recoiling)*: Not so loud, you'll wake the dead. Hold on, let me put in my ear. *(She rummages in her pocket)*

MINTY: Your "ear"?

MABEL: Ahh, here it is! *(She pops it in. It makes its high-pitched whine)*

MINTY: Ewww . . . doesn't it hurt?

MABEL: Hurt? Why would it hurt?

MINTY: That noise . . .

MABEL: It'll go away. *(It does)* See? *(Pause)* Where were we? Something about your father.

MINTY: I said he didn't see me in the play. He had to go to some conference in Switzerland. *(She starts swinging on Mabel's walker)*

MABEL: Well, he's a very important doctor.

MINTY: I like this walking thing. Can I play with it?

MABEL: Be my guest. *(To herself)* Oh for the eyes of a child!

MINTY: We haven't seen him in ages. It makes Mommy cry.

MABEL: He'll come to your next play.

MINTY: But I miss him!

MABEL: Then pretend he's there.

MINTY: Pretend?

MABEL: That's what I used to do when I swam. I'd imagine a crowd cheering me on. Family, friends, kings and queens . . . You can do it. You're a clever girl.

MINTY: Did it work?

MABEL: Every time. An imagination is a powerful thing.

MINTY: Mommy says you swam across the ocean.

MABEL: Not the ocean, the English Channel.

MINTY: *La Manche!* We just crossed it through the Chunnel.

MABEL: Smart girl! The water's frightfully cold, you know. At least it was back in 1928. There's only one way to insulate yourself against it. With grease and fat.

MINTY: Grease and fat?

MABEL: You smear on a ton of grease to keep you warm on the outside, and you gain all the weight you can to keep you warm on the inside.

MINTY: Ewwww!

MABEL: The more fat around you the better. Look at whales, they can stay in freezing water forever.

MINTY: I love whales.

MABEL: Me too.

MINTY: What do you do if you have to go the bathroom while you're swimming?

MABEL: You go. Who'll see?

MINTY: Ewwwww . . .

MABEL: It's quite pleasant, actually. Not unlike what I do now.

MINTY: *Ewwwww, ewwwww!*

MABEL: Wait till you're ninety!

(Silence.)

MINTY: Do you still swim?
MABEL: God, no.
MINTY: What do you do all day?
MABEL: I have no idea.

(Silence.)

MABEL: Do you know what a croquet set looks like?
MINTY: Sort of.
MABEL: Then how about looking for mine while you're up.
MINTY: Sure, where is it?
MABEL: Somewhere in that wretched closet.

(Minty disappears inside. There are a series of crashes.)

MABEL: Quietly, quietly, they'll kill us if we wake them up.

(Minty emerges with a mallet and ball.)

MINTY: Ta-da!
MABEL: Good girl!

(Minty hands the ball to Mabel and then swings the mallet.)

MINTY: Madame . . . ! It looks so funny.
MABEL: It's not funny in the least. Croquet is an extremely serious game. Have you ever played?
MINTY: Not really.
MABEL: Then I'll teach you how. See if you find some wickets.
MINTY (Disappearing into the closet): This is fun! There they are!

(There's a loud crash inside the closet.)

MABEL: Are you alright? Hello? *(Silence)* Minty, are you still alive?

MINTY: I think I broke something. *(She emerges with an impressive silver trophy that's missing a handle)*

MABEL: Well, well, what do you know?

MINTY: I'm sorry.

MABEL: My trophy for crossing the Channel.

MINTY: I'm sorry.

MABEL: God, I haven't seen that for years!

MINTY *(Starting to cry)*: I didn't mean to.

MABEL: There, there, it's alright.

MINTY: It just fell.

MABEL: It's not your fault, darling, it broke ages ago . . . Where were we? Oh yes, the wickets. How many did you find?

MINTY: Three. *(She returns to the closet to get them)*

MABEL: See if you can stick them in the floor. *(Indicating where)* There, there and there!

MINTY *(Crawling around with them)*: It's so dark, I can't see.

MABEL: If I turn on the light, it will wake everyone up. Just feel around for a space between the floorboards and push them in.

MINTY *(Pushing the first one in)*: Comme ça?

MABEL: Atta girl . . . Not too deep now, we have to be able to pull them out.

(Minty pushes in another one.)

MABEL: All we need is for Vita to come in and fall flat on her face!

MINTY *(Pushing in the last one)*: How's that?

MABEL: Perfect! There are nine wickets in all, but we'll just use these three. Now place the ball near the wicket and tap it through.

MINTY: OK . . . *(She prepares to take a mighty swing)*

MABEL: Take it easy now, we've got to be quiet.

MINTY *(Approaching the ball with more restraint)*: OK, here I go. Watch.

MABEL: I'm watching.

MINTY *(Hitting the ball through)*: I did it, I did it!

MABEL: Good girl! Keep going . . . But gently now.

MINTY: *Bien fait, Mignone. (She plays fitfully)*

MABEL: I used to love croquet. We had a gala tournament every Fourth of July. Everyone came. That's where I first fell in love with your great-grandfather . . . I was fourteen and he was nineteen. He was a friend of my brother, Phinney. Talk about handsome . . . I thought I'd faint as he came striding up the lawn. He had on his tennis whites and the sun was shining behind him, so he seemed to glow. He looked like something out of a fairy tale. He was barefoot for some reason . . . I'll never forget it. How pink his feet were against the freshly mown grass. It was as if they'd been painted they were so bright . . . Then he smiled this smile . . . The lawn started to tilt like a falling tea tray and everything flew upside down. Including him . . . He hovered over me like some fantastic flamingo with those blinding pink feet . . . I heard this pounding in my ears . . . The next thing I knew I was stretched out on a lawn chair and he was leaning over me, whispering, "May I have the next dance? May I have the next dance? May I have the next dance?" *(With a sigh)* Porter Bigelow . . . Be wary of handsome men, Minty, they're up to no good.

MINTY: I'll try to remember.

MABEL: Beauty and virtue rarely go together.

MINTY *(Preparing to make another shot)*: Watch Mou-Mou, watch!

MABEL: Particularly in men. I know . . . I learned the hard way.

(Minty hits the ball through the wicket.)

MABEL: Nice shot! You're quite an accomplished little player! Now do you see why I want to have a tournament out back? I don't know why everyone's giving me such a hard time.

MINTY: Grown-ups are strange.

MABEL: Grown-ups *are* strange. Particularly the ones around here. I've never seen such a bunch of pantywaists!

(Minty accidentally hits Mabel's foot with the ball.)

MABEL *(Crying out in pain)*: OW, OW!

MINTY *(Rushing over to her)*: Mou-Mou are you alright?

MABEL: My foot! My foot!

MINTY: I'm sorry . . .

MABEL: I told you to be careful!

MINTY *(Starting to cry)*: I didn't mean to.

MABEL *(With sudden rage)*: WHY CAN'T YOU PAY ATTENTION?!

MINTY *(Heading toward the door in tears)*: I'm sorry, I'm sorry . . .

VITA *(Suddenly appears)*: What's going on in here? I can't see! *(She turns on a light)*

MABEL: She hit me, she hit me! *(Groaning throughout)*

MINTY: I hit Mou-Mou in the foot by mistake.

JULIA *(Entering)*: Minty, what are you doing up at this hour?

VITA *(Rushing to Mabel)*: Are you alright?

MABEL *(Shrinking from Vita)*: Don't touch me!

VITA: Mrs. B., Mrs. B.? . . .

JULIA *(To Minty)*: Where did all these wickets come from?

VITA: What happened?

JULIA: What's been going on in here?

VITA *(Crouching by Mabel's foot)*: Let me see.

MABEL: Don't touch me!

VITA: I just want to look.

JULIA *(Calling)*: Minty, I asked you a question!

VITA: What are you doing with that trophy?

MABEL: Come one step closer and I'll scream.

JULIA *(To Minty)*: I'm not blind!

MABEL: I'm warning you.

VITA *(Trying to take the trophy away)*: Mrs. B. . . .

MABEL *(Clutching it for dear life)*: It's miiiiiiiiiine!

(This sudden harangue dovetails into another one that Mabel endured some fifty years before.)

Scene 2

April 1942. The living room of Mabel and Porter Bigelow's Boston townhouse. Like the Tidings's house, there's something oppressive about the place. Heavy carpets cover the floor and brocade drapes obscure the windows. The room is filled with family heirlooms and antiques. Grim-faced ancestors stare down from oil paintings. An imposing staircase is visible in the hall. Mabel, thirty-five, and Porter, forty-two, have just returned from a dinner party. Porter is drunk. He pours himself another drink as Mabel hangs up their coats offstage.

PORTER: You think I'm blind? You think I can't see? I asked you a question! You positively threw yourself at that fellow who claimed to know your English swimmer, what's-his-name . . . David Bernstein, Brustein, Blitzstein . . . *(Imitating her)* "You're a friend of David Blitzkrieg? How *is* he? I heard he joined the RAF and flew some very dangerous missions. He was shot down over the Channel? *Our* Channel? I can't listen! . . . He *survived*?! He had a picture of *me* next to his heart? Stop, stop, you mustn't tease!" I won't have it I tell you! I won't!

(Mabel enters wearing a stunning evening gown. Porter grabs her arm. They struggle.)

MABEL *(Wild)*: Stop it, stop it!

PORTER: You're my wife, *mine*!

EMMA'S VOICE *(From upstairs)*: Mummy, is that you?

MABEL: David Bloom is married with three children! And he's a doctor! He was never a flier!

EMMA'S VOICE *(Louder)*: *Mummy?*

PORTER: Great, you woke Emma. Billy will be next.

MABEL *(Calling to Emma)*: I'm alright, darling, go back to sleep.

PORTER: That's all we need . . .

MABEL *(To Emma)*: I thought I saw a mouse.

PORTER: *Both* children in tears.

MABEL: Billy sleeps through everything.

EMMA'S VOICE: Is Daddy there?

PORTER *(Under his breath)*: Jesus Christ!

MABEL: Yes, Daddy's here, everything's fine. Go back to sleep.

PORTER: This is a madhouse . . .

EMMA'S VOICE: Hi, Daddy.

PORTER: A lunatic asylum! *(Cheerful)* Hi, Emma.

EMMA'S VOICE: Did you get the mouse?

PORTER *(To Mabel)*: Mouse? What mouse?

MABEL *(To Emma)*: Yes, he got the mouse. Now go back to sleep, you have school tomorrow. Nighty-night. *(To Porter)* She's a light sleeper.

PORTER: Then why did you have to start screaming?

MABEL: Because you were about to hit me.

PORTER: *Hit* you? I'd never hit you.

MABEL: Do tell!

EMMA'S VOICE: Good night, Mummy.

MABEL: Good night, darling.

EMMA'S VOICE: Good night, Daddy.

PORTER: Good night, Emma.

MABEL: Thanks, Porter. Thanks a lot!

PORTER: Just one moment, *I'm* the wronged party here. It's one thing to carry a torch, but to *lash* yourself to it . . .

MABEL: I didn't say two words to that fellow.

PORTER: Ah, but the sighs that accompanied them!

MABEL: You're raving.

PORTER: I was there, darling.

MABEL: David and I are ancient history.

PORTER: I saw you!

MABEL: A flash in the pan.

PORTER: What does that actually *mean*: "A flash in the pan"? It sounds pretty torrid to me.

MABEL: I couldn't have done my swim without him.

PORTER *(Taking several gulps of his drink)*: Your swim, your swim . . . You'd think you crossed the Atlantic Ocean the way everyone carries on! Mabel Tidings's crossing and double-crossing. To Little Misery and back and what a misery it was. My bride to be, the pride of Pride's, the queen of tides and love that died . . . tossing and crossing with him at her side . . . How did she do it? Thirteen minutes and forty-two seconds!

MABEL: Hours! Thirteen *hours* . . .

PORTER: The American girl who swam the Channel with her English lover rowing beside her. It was so brazen, so romantic . . . I wish I could have been there. *(Putting on an English accent)* "Jolly good . . . stiff upper lip . . . keep going, old girl, and there'll be a nice fuck for you on the other side!"

MABEL: I don't have to listen to this!

PORTER: Why didn't you marry *him*? Doctor, world-class athlete, first in his class at Oxford . . . He had brains *and* brawn . . . a winning combination if ever there was one. Of course he was a Jew . . . Not that I have anything against the Jews. They're very capable people.

MABEL: You ought to hear yourself, it's frightening!

PORTER: I asked you a question. Why didn't you marry *him*?

MABEL: Porter, please . . .

PORTER: It was your chance to get out. You would have been the belle of Europe. Of course you *were* engaged . . .

MABEL: Darling . . .

PORTER: To *me*, as it happened. But you could have broken it off, you were resourceful.

MABEL: I beg of you!

EMMA'S VOICE *(From upstairs)*: Mummy, is that you?

PORTER: Of course our families would have hit the roof.

EMMA'S VOICE: Mummy?

PORTER: But better face a few weeks of unpleasantness than spend the rest of your life pining for him, but you didn't have the guts. Face it darling, you're still in love with him and always will be.

EMMA'S VOICE: *Mummy?*

MABEL *(Angrily to Emma)*: What is it, Emma?

EMMA'S VOICE: Did the mouse come back?

MABEL: This is torture, torture! *(To Emma)* Yes, it came back.

PORTER: I see how you clutch that trophy. *(Grabbing it off the mantel)*

EMMA'S VOICE: Where is it?

PORTER: Every time you touch it, it's like you're touching *him*! It's sickening, disgusting!

MABEL: Put that down!

PORTER: I won't have it, I tell you, I won't! *(He hurls it to the floor breaking off one of the handles)*

MABEL: No, no . . .

EMMA'S VOICE: Did you get the mouse?

MABEL *(To Porter)*: How could you? That was my trophy, *mine!*

PORTER *(Presenting it to her)*: Your funerary urn, madame, the ashes are still warm. *(To Emma)* Yes, Daddy got the mouse. Right in the kisser! *(To Mabel)* I need a drink.

MABEL: You've had enough.

PORTER *(Going to the bar)*: Try and stop me.

EMMA'S VOICE: May I come down and see it?

MABEL AND PORTER: *No, you may not come down and see it!*

EMMA'S VOICE: No fair, no fair.

PORTER *(To Emma)*: *Go to sleep!*

EMMA'S VOICE: I'm thirsty.

PORTER *(Pouring himself a drink)*: Care to join me?

(Silence.)

MABEL: I wasn't up to it.

PORTER: I beg your pardon?

MABEL: I lacked the courage.

PORTER: *You?*

MABEL: I was afraid I'd be swept away.

PORTER: I know the feeling.

MABEL: I couldn't live at that pitch.

PORTER *(Waving his arms)*: Help, I'm drowning . . . Help, hellllllllp!

MABEL: Somewhere between Dover and Calais I lost my nerve.

PORTER: A rope, a rope . . .

MABEL: He offered his hand, and I swam away. *Fool! Fool!*

(The clock starts striking twelve.)

MABEL: I often wonder what would have happened if I'd taken it.

PORTER: Well, you'd be living in the middle of a war, for one thing.

MABEL: And what pray tell, is *this?*

PORTER: A husband expressing concern over his wife.

MABEL: Night after night after night after night . . . I can't take it anymore!

PORTER: I don't see any dead bodies.

MABEL: I said: *I can't take it!*

PORTER: I'm sorry darling, I don't know what came over me.

MABEL: You know perfectly well what came over you. It comes over you every night.

PORTER: You're my world. I adore you!

MABEL: You're going to kill yourself.

PORTER *(Trying to embrace her)*: Your face, your eyes, your lips, your tongue . . .

MABEL: The drinking has got to stop!

PORTER: It will, I promise. I give you my word.

MABEL: Your word, your word . . .

PORTER: My nymph, my bucking sea horse . . .

MABEL: *I'm sick to death of your words!*

(A pause.)

PORTER: How about my smile, then? *(He throws her a weak smile)*

MABEL *(Turning to go)*: I'm tired. I'm going to bed.

PORTER: Don't leave me!

MABEL *(Heading for the stairs)*: I'll be in Billy's room.

PORTER: M. T., M. T. . . . Come back . . .

(Mabel slowly climbs the stairs as Porter reaches out for her.)

SCENE 3

The present. Mabel's bedroom on the Fourth of July, around noon. Julia and Minty are in their slips, looking through Granny Tidings's lawn dresses. The rejects lie on Mabel's bed. Julia spies an especially elegant dress and holds it up to herself in front of the mirror.

JULIA: Oh Minty, look at this one!

MINTY: Go for it!

JULIA: Dress number . . . *four*! *(Putting it on)* Come, help me get into it.

MINTY: Ewww, that smell . . .

JULIA: Good old mothballs. Careful, careful, it's very fragile. *(Twirling around)* What do you think?

MINTY: You look like a bride.

JULIA: Yeah?

MINTY: That's the one.

JULIA: I don't know about the sleeves.

MINTY: What's wrong with them?

JULIA: They make my arms look fat.

MINTY: No, they don't,

JULIA *(Selecting another dress)*: What about this?

MINTY: It's awful!

JULIA: It *is* awful!

MINTY: The one you have on is perfect. Now *I* have to find one.

JULIA (*Posing in front of the mirror*): I can't get over what great condition they're in.

MINTY (*Looking through the rejects*): Everything's so big.

(*The doorbell rings.*)

MABEL (*From the living room*): I've got it, I've got it!

MINTY: Oh no, they're here! (*She frantically looks through the dresses and starts putting one on*)

MABEL: Kitty! Come in, come in! We're in the bedroom.

(*Mabel and Kitty Lowell enter. Mabel's in a rumpled house dress and Kitty, ninety-one, wears a flowered dress she's had for years.*)

MABEL (*To Kitty*): You remember my granddaughter, Julia, don't you?

KITTY (*To Julia*): My, my, don't you look elegant! Just like a bride.

JULIA (*To Minty*): Maybe Mou-Mou will let you borrow one of these when *you* get married.

MABEL: Take your pick.

MINTY: It's a deal.

MABEL: And *that's* my favorite great-grandchild, Mignone, whom we call Minty for some reason.

(*Everyone looks at Minty who is swimming in one of Granny Tidings's lawn dresses.*)

JULIA (*Laughing*): Minty!

KITTY: Of course, I remember you!

MABEL: You look like an angel! An ornament on top of a Christmas tree.

(*A pause.*)

JULIA (*Under her breath to Minty*): Embrace-la, petite.

(Minty kisses Kitty on both cheeks.)

KITTY: Heaven, heaven!

MABEL: Isn't she divine? Alright, Kitty, off with your dress and on with one of Granny Tidings's.

KITTY: And what if I don't want to?

JULIA: There's no arguing with her.

KITTY: We've been friends for over eighty years. You'd think I'd be able to stand up for myself by now.

MABEL *(Clapping her hands)*: Chop, chop, let's get moving!

KITTY: But she barks, and I jump. It's pathetic. *(She takes off her dress)*

MABEL *(Caressing Kitty's cheek)*: It's not pathetic, it's very endearing.

JULIA: Minty, that dress swims on you!

MINTY *(Strutting around, putting on airs)*: "Harold and I would like more tea, Jeeves!"

MABEL *(To Kitty)*: She's going to be an actress when she grows up.

MINTY: "There's nothing like a quiet evening at home to dispel the shocks and disappointments of the day!"

(Mabel and Kitty laugh as Minty shimmies out of the dress.)

MABEL: It's such a shame Vita couldn't be here. Her father suddenly died, so she and West had to fly to Florida for the funeral. Don't ask me where she got the fare. The woman thinks money grows on trees!

(The doorbell rings.)

MABEL: Julia, would you?

JULIA *(Exiting)*: I'm on my way!

MABEL: Come on Kitty, we don't have all day.

(Kitty starts looking through the dresses.)

JULIA (*At the door*): Come in, come in. We're all in the bedroom)

(*Julia ushers in Chandler Coffin, dressed in a splendid white linen suit, and Wheels and Pinky Wheelock. Wheels is ninety-three and very doddery. He's also dressed in white, but is nowhere near as elegant as Chandler. His wife, Pinky, ninety-three, is dressed in her usual pink.*)

MABEL: Happy Fourth of July!

CHANDLER, WHEELS AND PINKY: Happy Fourth of July to you too!

(*Kitty and Minty squeal at being caught in their slips and cover themselves.*)

MINTY AND KITTY: Don't come in! We're dressing!

CHANDLER (*Retreating to the door*): I don't think Wheels and I belong in here.

MABEL: Fiddlesticks! We're too old to be modest!

KITTY (*Clutching one of Granny Tidings's dresses up to herself*): Speak for yourself. The Lowells aren't flesh mongers!

MABEL AND PINKY: *Kitty!*

MINTY: "Flesh mongers"? *Qu'est-ce que c'est?*

CHANDLER (*Linking arms with Wheels*): We're on our way.

WHEELS (*Resisting*): Not so fast . . .

CHANDLER: The ladies want to be alone!

WHEELS (*Lingering*): Now don't wear something too risqué, Pinky, I'm ninety-three with a weak heart!

MABEL: Don't worry, we'll keep an eye on her!

WHEELS (*To Pinky*): If you need me for anything, I'll be right outside the door.

CHANDLER (*Pulling him out of the room*): Come along, Wheels.

WHEELS (*Under his breath*): Spoilsport!

*(Pinky starts shimmying out of her dress, humming a
stripper tune.)*

JULIA: Go, Mrs. Wheelock!
MABEL: That's our Pinky!
KITTY: Fastest girl in Miss Windsor's school!
MABEL: Fastest girl on *Beacon Hill*!
MINTY: Me, too, me, too! *(She starts imitating Pinky)*
JULIA: Easy, Minty, easy . . . You'll rip your dress!

> *(They all whistle and applaud as Pinky tosses her dress
> to the floor with a saucy bump and grind.)*

WHEELS *(Popping his head in)*: What's going on in there?
PINKY: Nothing for *your* eyes!
KITTY: Out, out!
CHANDLER *(Peeking in, under the guise of pulling Wheels
   back)*: You heard them Wheels!
KITTY: You too, Chan!

> *(They retreat, singing the stripper tune that Pinky was
> humming. Silence.)*

MINTY: Men!
KITTY *(Holding a dress up to herself)*: What do you think?
MABEL: It's scrumptious! Try it on. Come on Pinky, you're
   next.
JULIA: What about you?
MABEL: Guests have first choice. I'll take what's left.

> *(Kitty, Pinky and Minty start trying on dresses.)*

KITTY: Help me, Julia, I can't find the buttons.
JULIA *(Assisting her)*: No wonder—half of them have
   fallen off.
MINTY *(Whirling around in her dress, pretending to be
   Cinderella)*: How can I thank you, Fairy Godmother?
   I'll be the most beautiful girl at the ball.

PINKY: Just remember to leave at midnight or all bets are off!

KITTY *(Striking a pose)*: How do we look?

(Pinky and Minty join her. They look preposterous.)

MABEL: You have to switch! Pinky wear Kitty's! Kitty wear Minty's! And Minty look for another one!

(They look at each other and realize she's right.)

MABEL *(Clapping her hands)*: Chop, chop, we don't have all day.

(They start undressing.)

WHEELS *(Near the door)*: It's awfully quiet in there. *(He pops his head in again)*

| MABEL: | PINKY: | KITTY: | JULIA: |
| Wheels?! | Behave yourself! | Out, out! | Mr. Wheelock! |

(Wheels ducks out of view.)

PINKY: You'd think he was a teenager!

(They start switching dresses in slow motion.)

MABEL: Now *I'd* better look for something. *(She pulls out a stylish black hat with a veil)* Good God! The hat I wore to Porter's funeral. And the program from the service. What are they doing in here? *(She puts on the hat and reads the program)* "In memoriam, Porter Ransom Bigelow, August 17, 1900 to April 2, 1967, King's Chapel, Boston, Massachusetts." Poor Porter . . . His cancer consumed him like a threshing machine, but he never made a peep. No complaints, no regrets.

He bore it like a Trojan . . . How did those wonderful words at his funeral go? "What a chimera then is man! What a novelty! What a monster, what a chaos, what a contradiction . . ."

(Mabel's voice dovetails with Dr. Peabody's as she is transported back to Porter's funeral, thirty years before.)

Scene 4

King's Chapel, Boston, 1967. Mabel, sixty, is the only mourner who's visible, though it's clear from the sound she's not alone. The turnout is small, however, only thirty-five people. Dr. Peabody's service is coming to an end.

DR. PEABODY: ". . . What a novelty! What a monster, what a chaos, what a contradiction, what a prodigy! Judge of all things, feeble earthworm, depository of truth, a sink of uncertainty and error, the glory and the shame of the universe." *(He pauses)* ". . . Let us bow our heads and pray. 'Our Father who art in Heaven . . .'"

THE CONGREGATION:
". . . Hallowed be thy name.
Thy kingdom come, thy will be done
On earth as it is in Heaven.
Give us this day our daily bread,
And forgive us our trespasses
As we forgive those who trespass against us.
And lead us not into temptation
But deliver us from evil.
For thine is the kingdom, and the power and the glory.
For ever and ever,
Amen."

DR. PEABODY: *(Arms raised)*: "The Lord bless you and keep you. The Lord make his face to shine upon you,

and be gracious unto you. The Lord lift up his counte-
nance upon you, and give you peace."
THE CONGREGATION: Amen.

*(Bach's organ prelude, Liebster Jesu wir sind hier, s. 706,
plays. Sound effect of the mourners leaving. Mabel
remains in the front row, staring into space. A woman in
black tentatively approaches her.)*

MABEL *(Turning around)*: Who's there? Who is that?
PRU: It's me, Pru.
MABEL: Pru?
PRU: Prudence O'Neill, your old serving girl.
MABEL: I'm sorry, I'm afraid I don't . . .
PRU: *Mary's* daughter! You remember. We used to watch
   you swim.
MABEL: Pru, *Pru!*
PRU: Yes, Miss . . .
MABEL: I don't believe it!
PRU: I mean, ma'am.
MABEL: Look at you!
PRU *(Under her breath)*: I mean, Mrs. Bigelow.
MABEL: You're all grown-up!
PRU: It's got to be what? Forty years!
MABEL: Darling Pru! *(She gazes at her enrapt and then
   thumps the seat beside her)* Sit down, sit down.
PRU *(Hanging back)*: I don't want to intrude.
MABEL: *Pru!* You could knock me over with a feather!
PRU *(Remains standing)*: It was a lovely service.
MABEL: A bit long.
PRU: I've never been in a Unitarian church before.
MABEL: Well, you know the old joke: The only time you
   hear the name Jesus Christ in a Unitarian church is
   when the janitor falls down the stairs.
PRU *(Bursts out laughing)*: Miss, Miss . . .
MABEL: You've never heard that before?

PRU (*Wiping her eyes*): No one can make me laugh like you. I'm sorry, I'm sorry . . .

MABEL: No, no, it's good to laugh.

PRU: But not at your husband's funeral, Miss. Mr. Bigelow was such a lovely boy. I mean, fine man.

(*A pause.*)

MABEL: Pru, Pru, tell me everything! Your dear mother?

PRU: She died just last August.

MABEL: I'm so sorry.

PRU: Heart failure.

MABEL: Poor Mary!

PRU: She went very fast.

MABEL: And your father? (*Trying to remember his name*) Uh . . . uh . . .

PRU AND MABEL: *Norton!*

MABEL: Mama always said he was the best chauffeur we ever had.

PRU: He died years ago.

MABEL: No!

PRU: Shortly after your mother.

MABEL: When was that? I have no memory.

PRU: 1952.

MABEL: Where does time go?

PRU: The same year my Annie got married.

MABEL: You have children?

PRU: Six.

MABEL: *Six?!*

PRU: And ten grandchildren!

MABEL: Good grief!

PRU: And you?

MABEL: Two children and two grandchildren. (*Pause*) The turnout was pathetic.

PRU: I beg your pardon?

MABEL (*Looking around*): Only thirty-five people showed up. If that!

PRU: It was more like seventy, I'd say.

MABEL: Well, who likes going to funerals?

PRU: I was in the back, I had a better view.

(Silence.)

MABEL *(In a sudden burst)*: And did you marry Buddy?

PRU: Buddy?

MABEL: The young man who drove the train. *(She pulls the imaginary whistle)* Whoo-oo.

PRU *(Laughing again)*: Saints preserve us!

MABEL: Well, did you?

PRU: No, Miss, I mean ma'am . . . I married Freddy Fitzgerald.

MABEL *(With a twinkle)*: And what, pray tell, does Freddy drive?

PRU *(World-weary)*: *Me*, I'm afraid.

MABEL: Men!

PRU: "They're either devils or fools."

MABEL: "Better marry a fool than share a devil with forty-two wives."

MABEL AND PRU *(Chanting)*:
"Patrick McCann, Patrick McCann,
forty-three rings on forty-three hands."

(They laugh and are suddenly quiet.)

PRU *(Shifting on her feet)*: Well, you'll want to be joining your family.

MABEL *(Rising)*: Dearest Pru, you were so good to come.

PRU: Not at all. I wanted to pay my respects.

(They walk up the aisle together.)

MABEL: And have you been happy?

PRU: *Happy?*

MABEL: Yes.

PRU: Have *you?*

MABEL *(Beginning to cheer up)*: When I least expect it.

PRU *(With a sigh)*: Like everything else.

MABEL *(Flinging her arms around her with joy)*: Darling Pru . . . I've missed you so!

PRU *(Hanging on for dear life)*: I've missed you too. More than you'll ever know.

(The lights fade on their embrace.)

Scene 5

The present. Mabel's Fourth of July party is underway beneath a sparkling blue sky. The guests stand frozen in various attitudes of play—the women, elegant in Granny Tidings's lawn dresses; the men, courtly in their old linen suits. The whiteness of their clothes is brilliant against the green of the grass and overarching trees. It looks like a Sargent painting come to life. No one moves.

CHANDLER *(Calling toward the house)*: Hurry up, M. T., we can't hold these poses forever.

KITTY: That woman can get us to do anything!

PINKY: A group photo at our age. What next? A slumber party, no doubt!

WHEELS: I'm getting a muscle spasm in my leg.

CHANDLER: I feel like one of the nymphs forever frozen on Keat's Grecian Urn.

"Thou, silent form, dost tease us out of thought
As doth eternity: Cold Pastoral!"

MINTY: *I* think it's fun!

KITTY *(Running her hands over her bodice)*: What I can't get over is that we actually *fit* in these old things.

(Julia pushes Mabel onstage in a wheelchair. She, too, is wearing one of Granny Tidings's lawn dresses. Vita's Paul Revere hat is perched on her head.)

MABEL: Success, success, I found the camera! It was buried under my darning.

KITTY:	CHANDLER:	PINKY:	WHEELS:	MINTY:
Good God!	There's that hat again!	Look at that hat!	Nice hat!	Yes!

CHANDLER: Not Paul Revere again!

MABEL: Vita was going to wear it, leading the Fourth of July parade. On horseback, if you please.

KITTY: She's an original alright.

MABEL: Since she couldn't be here, I thought I'd do the honors. Let's see a little patriotism, for God's sake! Julia's going to take our picture.

KITTY: But we look a hundred years old in these things.

MABEL: On the contrary, you look very handsome. Like a Sargent painting come to life! *(Handing Julia the camera)* Darling . . . *(To the others)* Let's see those mallets now!

(They raise their mallets and pose.)

JULIA *(Looking at them through the camera)*: She's right. You should see yourselves. It's amazing! Alright everyone, scrunch together.

(They do.)

PINKY *(Poking Wheels in the ribs)*: Look lively, Wheels!

WHEELS *(A million miles away)*: Hmmm?

PINKY: Julia's going to take our picture.

WHEELS: Right you are, right you are. *(He strikes a commanding pose)*

JULIA: Say "money!"

ALL EXCEPT WHEELS: Money!

(They break the pose.)

WHEELS: Money!

JULIA: That was great!

MABEL: Did you get me from my good side?

JULIA (*Handing her the camera back, world-weary*): Yes, I got you from your good side.

MABEL: Thank you darling, you're a saint! (*She makes her lurid kissing sound and sits in the seat of honor*) Ugh!

(*Silence.*)

PINKY: What a day!

KITTY: Perfection!

CHANDLER: Well, M. T., you've done it again.

MABEL: Hmmm?

CHANDLER: I said, *you've done it again!*

MABEL: What did I do?

CHANDLER (*With a sweeping gesture*): This!

MABEL: I can only take credit for the food, you have to thank the man upstairs for everything else.

KITTY: The food was divine. As always.

MABEL: It's all Vita's doing. It's such a pity her father had to drop dead last night. Oh well, "*L'homme propose, Dieu dispose!*"

PINKY (*Glancing at Wheels, who's fallen asleep in his chair*): WHEELS, ARE YOU STILL ALIVE? (*Starts shaking him*) Sweetheart?

KITTY: Poor Wheels.

MABEL: Poor Wheels.

CHANDLER: "There but for the grace of God, go I."

KITTY: Wake up!

CHANDLER: Remember Snap Sessions?

CHANDLER, MABEL, PINKY AND KITTY: Dropped dead during Dr. Cummings's sermon on original sin.

CHANDLER: Pitched face forward into Tippy Loring and was gone.

MABEL: Poor thing thought he was trying to kiss her!

(They laugh and laugh.)

KITTY: I always liked Tippy. She was a great reader you know. She could recite entire chapters of Gibbon's *Decline and Fall of the Roman Empire* by heart.

MABEL: Gone, gone . . . We're all that's left.

CHANDLER:
"Oh build your ship of death, your little ark
and furnish it with food, with little cakes, and wine
for the dark flight down oblivion."

MABEL, KITTY AND PINKY: D. H. Lawrence.

CHANDLER: D. H. Lawrence.

(Silence.)

PINKY *(Shaking Wheels)*: Come on, Wheels . . . Open those baby blues . . .

MABEL: Oh, let him sleep.

PINKY: But I miss him. *(Shaking him harder)* Wheels? WHEELS?

MINTY: Is he alright?

PINKY: He's fine. It's just a condition he has.

KITTY: What's it called? Necrophilia?

CHANDLER: That's sleeping with a dead person!

PINKY: Narcolepsy.

MABEL, CHANDLER AND KITTY: *Narcolepsy!*

MINTY: *He's dead, he's dead!*

MABEL: *Minty!*

PINKY *(Shaking him hard)*: SWEETHEART, YOU'RE SCARING US!

WHEELS *(Waking with a jolt)*: Hmm? What?

PINKY: You fell asleep again.

WHEELS: What's that?

PINKY: I SAID, YOU FELL ASLEEP!

MINTY: That was neat. Do it again, do it again!

MABEL: Alright everybody, let's get this show on the road!

(All but Minty groan.)

MABEL: This is a croquet party, in case you've forgotten!

ALL BUT MINTY: We're too old!

MABEL: Excuses, excuses . . . COME ON WHEELS, UP AND AT 'EM!

PINKY: Count us out.

MABEL: Alright . . . Julia and Minty against Kitty and Chandler, then.

KITTY: Heaven help us.

CHANDLER: You'd better be ready to call 911.

MINTY: What about you, Mou-Mou?

MABEL: I can't walk, in case you haven't noticed.

MINTY: You don't have to walk. Watch.

(Minty props herself against the walker and swings her mallet.)

CHANDLER:	KITTY:	PINKY:	WHEELS:
Good job!	Look at her go!	Bravo!	Nicely done!

JULIA: Go for it, Grand!

MABEL *(Ignoring them)*: Enough of this foolishness! Chan, will you do the honors and go first?

CHANDLER: Do I have to?

MABEL *(Clapping her hands)*: *Allez-y, allez-y!*

KITTY: Talk about *déjà vu.* That's the same set your parents used to have.

MABEL: Come on, Chan, I've never seen such a bunch of pantywaists. You only live once!

CHANDLER: Alright, alright . . .

(He gets on the course and hits the ball through the first wicket.)

ALL: Good shot! Nicely done! Bravo! Well done! Good going!

(Chandler keeps playing.)

MABEL: Look at him, our dashing poet laureate.

CHANDLER: "Poet," but hardly "dashing" or "laureate" . . .
A minor talent at best.

MABEL: Now, now . . .

KITTY: All the ladies wanted to be your partner.

PINKY: Remember how we fought over him?

KITTY: Tooth and nail.

MABEL: Hammer and tongs.

PINKY: But he only had eyes for M. T.

MABEL: Please!

CHANDLER *(Misses his shot)*: Rats!

MINTY *(Running onto the court)*: Can I go next?

MABEL: You mean, "may" I? Yes, you may.

MINTY: Watch, Mom.

JULIA: I'm watching.

MINTY: Here I go. *(She taps the ball through the first wicket)*
I did it! I did it!

ALL: Good girl! Bravo! Nice shot! The girl's a natural!

MABEL: Hit it again, you get two more turns.

MINTY: Watch, Mom.

PINKY: Just like our great-grandchildren. God help you if
you take your eyes off them for a second.

MABEL: They want their accomplishments seen.

MINTY *(Preparing to swing)*: Here I go . . .

MABEL: The maids used to watch me swim. I couldn't
have crossed the Channel without them.

MINTY *(Hits the ball but misses the wicket)*: Phooey.

ALL: Too bad. Nice try. Next time . . .

MABEL: You're quite a little player . . . Alright Kitty, you're
up next.

KITTY *(Grabbing a mallet)*: "We who are about to die,
salute you!"

CHANDLER: "Hail Caesar, all hail!"

(Kitty taps the ball through.)

KITTY *(Doing a little bump and grind)*: Mother pin a rose on me!

PINKY: M. T. how come you and Chan didn't marry each other? It would have made such sense!

MABEL AND CHANDLER: *Pinky?!*

KITTY: She's right, it would have made sense.

PINKY: You look so handsome together.

MABEL *(To Chandler)*: Just ignore them.

PINKY: I never understood what you saw in Porter Bigelow.

KITTY: That damn smile.

PINKY: But he was a drunk.

MABEL: I think this conversation has gone far enough.

KITTY *(Misses her shot)*: Damn! *(She sits down)*

JULIA: My turn, my turn!

(Julia plays in silence.)

CHANDLER: She wouldn't have me.

MABEL: What did I know?

CHANDLER: You knew you didn't want me.

MABEL: You never choose the right person when you're young.

CHANDLER: Some of us never even choose the wrong one.

KITTY: I married Sarge because he was the first one who asked me. God, I miss him!

PINKY: And I married Wheels because he said yes.

KITTY: *You* proposed?

PINKY: I knew he was the one for me the moment I laid eyes on him. I popped the question on a Wednesday and we were married by Sunday! *(She jabs Wheels in the ribs)* Come on Wheels, wake up!

WHEELS *(Wakes like a shot)*: Right you are, right you are!

PINKY: Isn't he darling?

KITTY: And then some.

MABEL: A real prize.

CHANDLER: And quite the golfer in his day.

(Silence as everyone gazes at Wheels.)

WHEELS: What did I do?

PINKY: Nothing. You just *are*!

KITTY, MABEL AND CHANDLER: Awww . . .

(Silence.)

KITTY *(To Mabel)*: M. T., can I ask you a question? I know it's none of my business, but I've always wanted to know. What happened between you and that English swimmer . . . David something . . .

CHANDLER: Bloom.

PINKY: Yes, what *did* happen?

KITTY: I remember seeing his picture in the paper after your swim. He was *very* attractive!

PINKY: A dream!

KITTY: Wasn't he a doctor or something?

CHANDLER: An obstetrician.

KITTY: And didn't he swim the Channel the year before you?

CHANDLER: Fourteen hours and eighteen minutes.

KITTY: You seem to know an awful lot about this fellow, Chan.

CHANDLER: Well, I spent a good three weeks with him.

KITTY AND PINKY: You *did*?

CHANDLER: I was M. T.'s trainer, remember? Wherever she went, I went.

KITTY: Of course, I forgot!

(Silence as everyone gazes at him.)

CHANDLER: They met at the Channel Swimmers' Association. It was love at first sight.

KITTY: Then why didn't you marry?

(Everyone looks at Mabel.)

MABEL: Why is everyone so interested in David Bloom all of a sudden?

KITTY: Because we want to know what happened.

JULIA: You're always so elusive about him.

MABEL: It's none of your business!

JULIA: It's like you're ashamed or something.

MABEL: *Ashamed?* Why would I be ashamed?

KITTY: Because he was . . . you know . . .

MABEL: No, I *don't* know. Please enlighten me.

(Silence.)

KITTY: Jewish. *(Pause)* There. I said it.

MABEL: You think *that's* why?

CHANDLER *(Under his breath)*: Here we go . . .

KITTY: Well, it's stopped plenty of girls before you.

PINKY: I never went out with a Jew. My father would have disowned me.

KITTY: I did.

PINKY, WHEELS, MABEL AND CHANDLER: You *did?*

KITTY: Well, he was half Jewish. Alfred Nightingale.

PINKY: *I* remember him! He was very attractive.

KITTY: But then I met Sarge and the rest is history.

PINKY: Alfred Nightingale. I haven't heard that name in years!

(Silence.)

MABEL: You're right, I *was* ashamed. Of *myself!* I wasn't up to him.

THE OTHERS: Up to him?

MABEL: He was a force of nature. A typhoon, a tidal wave . . .

JULIA: Like Jean-Paul.

MABEL: I didn't know what hit me.

JULIA: You swam the Channel, nonetheless.

MABEL: But I couldn't keep going. You, on the other hand, reached the distant shore. That's why I admire you so.

JULIA: Please . . .

MABEL: You stayed your course.

JULIA *(Suddenly swamped with sadness)*: I stayed my course.

MINTY *(Sidling up to her)*: Hi, Mommy.

JULIA: Hello, darling.

MINTY: Are you OK?

(Silence as Julia considers.)

JULIA *(Perking up)*: Of course I'm OK. And do you know why?

(Minty waits.)

JULIA *(Hugging her)*: Because *you're* with me. My dearest precious Minty, I love you so! My treasure, my heart's delight! *(She kisses her)*

THE OTHERS: Awww . . .

MINTY *(Embarrassed)*: Mom!

JULIA *(Disentangling herself)*: Sorry, sorry, I'll behave.

(Silence.)

MABEL *(To Julia)*: You went the distance, but not me . . . Oh no . . . I pulled myself together and turned back. I did the right and proper thing. I followed the rules. *Fool, fool! (She rises, grabbing a mallet)*

JULIA *(Rushing to her side)*: Grand? What do you think you're doing?

MABEL *(Hitting a ball)*: Playing croquet! What does it look like I'm doing?

MINTY: *Yes!*

KITTY AND THE WHEELOCKS: But it's not your turn.

CHANDLER: And it's not your ball.

MABEL: I don't care!

MINTY *(At Mabel's side)*: May I be on your team?

MABEL: There are no teams, it's every man for himself!
(She hits another ball)

MINTY: Wait for me! *(Hits her ball)*

JULIA: Nice shot!

MABEL: That's my girl!

MINTY: Again, again! *(Repeatedly hits her ball)*

CHANDLER: What about the rules?

MABEL: The rules, the rules . . . I'm sick to death of the rules! *(Hitting a ball through a wicket)* Come on, everyone play at once!

KITTY: Hey, that was my ball!

CHANDLER *(To Mabel)*: What's come over you?

MINTY *(Laying her ball at her feet)*: Here's yours, Mou-Mou.

MABEL: Thank you, darling.

CHANDLER: This is a civilized game.

MABEL: And as with all civilizations, things change. It's called *progress.*

CHANDLER: But how will we know who wins?

MABEL: Who cares?

CHANDLER: I care! I was winning,

MABEL: For God's sake, Chan, we've walked out of the Dark Ages into the light of day! *(Hitting her ball)* Come on Wheelocks get out there!

WHEELS *(Waking up)*: What's that?

PINKY: M. T. wants us to play.

MABEL: *Insists* you play!

PINKY: All at the same time, if you please.

WHEELS: Sounds good to me. Lead me to the course.

(Pinky takes his arm and leads him to the first wicket.)

MABEL: I knew I could count on you.

PINKY: Alright, Wheels, the wicket's right in front of you.

WHEELS: Stand back, here I go! *(He whacks the ball)* Did it go through?

PINKY:	KITTY:	MINTY:
Straight as an arrow!	Unbelievable!	Go, Mr Wheelock!

CHANDLER: This is a travesty!

WHEELS: You're just jealous because I'm so good! *(He hits the ball through the next wicket)*

MABEL: Come on, Chan, or you'll be left behind.

CHANDLER *(Striding out onto the course)*: Alright, alright, but I don't approve. You have no respect for the game. *(He hits the ball)*

(They all play at once, getting increasingly reckless.)

JULIA *(Singing)*: "Allons enfants, de la patrie . . ." *(She hits the ball)*

MINTY *(Singing)*: "La jour de gloire est arrivée . . ." *(She hits the ball)*

MABEL *(Stops in her tracks, seeing her hallucination again)*: The horses are massing on the shore. Look at them go! Heads tossing, manes flying . . .

CHANDLER:
"Turning and turning in the widening gyre
The falcon cannot hear the falconer . . ."
(He hits the ball)
"Things fall apart; the center cannot hold;
Mere anarchy is loosed upon the world . . ."

(He hits the ball.)

PINKY *(To Wheels)*: Hey, you knocked mine into the bushes. *(She exits, looking for her ball)*

KITTY *(Hitting the ball)*: "Once more unto the breach, dear friends, once more . . ."

MABEL: They stamp their feet, plunging into the waves.

CHANDLER: Watch it, Kitty, that was my ball!

MABEL *(Weaving across the lawn)*: Wait for me, wait for me . . .

MINTY: Look out, Mommy, I'm going to get you!

(A cacophony of voices speaking in English accents mingles with the shouts of the players: "I'll drop you off here,

there's no easy access to Shakespeare Beach."... "I know, thank you very much."... "Good luck with your swim. An American girl did it last year, you know, but from France to England."... "Hurry up, we only have a quarter of an hour."... "What's your name again?"... "Come on M. T., the world awaits," etc., as:)

CHANDLER: *(Finally noticing Mabel)*: M. T. what are you doing?

(Everyone freezes.)

MABEL *(Staggers away from them, paddling her arms)*: I'm coming, David. I'm coming . . .

(The voices from the past get louder and louder. We hear the cawing of gulls and the slap of waves against the shore.)

Scene 6

August 1928, Shakespeare Beach, off the Cliffs of Dover, England. It's 4:30 in the morning and still dark. Sea gulls are cawing and the cliffs are shrouded in fog. Mabel, twenty-one, is preparing for her swim. The legendary English swimmer, David Bloom, late twenties, stands beside her.

DAVID *(Opening a jar of lanolin)*: Alright, M. T., time to grease up. Human beings weren't meant to go swimming in fifty-eight–degree water. Sea lions and polar bears perhaps, but not scrawny young women.

MABEL: I'm not scrawny. I'm at my optimum weight!

DAVID: Speaking of animals that take to the water, did you know that the Bengal tiger swims up to fourteen miles when it crosses the Java Sea to breed in Borneo. *(Kissing her neck and arms)* My lovely beast, my elegant cat . . .

MABEL: David . . .

DAVID *(Smearing lanolin all over her)*:
"Tyger, Tyger! burning bright,
In the forests of the night."

MABEL *(Pulling away)*: Uuugh, it smells!

DAVID: Hold still.

MABEL: You added something.

DAVID: Porpoise oil.

MABEL: Porpoise oil?

DAVID: It helps keep the jellyfish off.

MABEL: Don't speak to me about jellyfish!

DAVID: I also added paraffin.

MABEL *(Thrusting out her arms)*: Look at these stings I got yesterday!

DAVID *(Greasing her up between kisses)*: Lanolin, porpoise oil, paraffin and kisses. I dare them to come near you! Nervous?

MABEL: No. *(Pause)* How odd.

DAVID: It's not odd at all, you're in top form.

MABEL: You think?

DAVID: You could swim the Atlantic Ocean.

(The sky gradually gets lighter.)

MABEL: Shouldn't the pilot boat be here soon?

DAVID *(Checking his watch)*: It's not five yet.

MABEL: Look at that fog. It's even thicker than yesterday.

DAVID: There's always fog in the Dover Straits. Weather conditions are perfect. You couldn't ask for better winds.

MABEL: I wish I'd known you when you did it. You broke every record.

DAVID: Luck. Sheer luck.

MABEL: Fourteen hours and eighteen minutes!

DAVID: A south-west tidal stream carried me the last two miles, I didn't have to swim a stroke. I was literally washed onto *Cap Griz Nez*. Like Moses among the bull rushes—*drawn from the water*. That's what Moses means, in case you're interested . . .

MABEL: Drawn from the water?

DAVID: It's not unlike delivering babies, come to think of it. I draw them from their amniotic fluid.

MABEL: I can't even *imagine* delivering a baby.

DAVID: Someday I'll bring you along.

MABEL: Not on your life! *(Taking him in)* David, David, you've been so wonderful. I wouldn't be standing here if it weren't for you.

DAVID: That's not true, Chandler trained you very well.

MABEL: Poor Chandler.

DAVID: He's in love with you, you know.

MABEL: He wanted to accompany me so badly, but then I met you. Am I heartless?

DAVID: Utterly.

MABEL: I'm so happy, I've never been so happy!

DAVID: You're magnificent! Like a sunset, an avalanche, a starry night . . . Run away with me. After the swim . . . When we reach France . . .

MABEL: But what about Porter Bigelow?

DAVID: What about him?

MABEL: We're engaged.

DAVID: Then break it off.

MABEL: It would kill him.

DAVID: And what about you?

MABEL: I made a promise.

DAVID: But not a vow! There's a difference.

MABEL: How could I face him again? Or our families?

DAVID: You'd never have to. You'd be with me.

MABEL: But we grew up together.

DAVID: And now you're free to come and go as your choose. *(Taking her in his arms)* Listen to me, darling. I know I sound impulsive, but once in a while something miraculous happens. You're swimming along and the love of your life drops down beside you. He holds out his hand . . . Or is it a wing? . . . and says, "Follow me." You have a split second to decide. Will you stay your course or take it? *(He starts kissing her)*

MABEL: David, David . . .

DAVID: Come with me, we'll leave the sadness of the world and swim the seven seas. We'll start in the Mediterranean, travel overland to the Red Sea, round the Gulf of Aden, pick up the Arabian Sea and follow the coast of India till we hit the Bay of Bengal . . . Then it's due south to Sumatra, the South China Sea and, finally, the Coral Sea, ringed with doves and hummingbirds . . .

MABEL: Stop, stop . . .

DAVID: We'll live on starfish, minnows and snails. Our bodies will fuse and we'll be absorbed into each other, like a fabulous sea anemone—phylum: *Cnidaria*, genus: *Stoichactis*, distant cousin of the passionflower . . .

MABEL: David, please . . .

DAVID: Phylum: *Passiflora*; species: *incarnata*.

MABEL: Oh God . . . Oh God . . .

DAVID: You didn't know I could speak Latin, did you? I can also throw a javelin, shear a sheep and walk on hot coals.

(The lights of the pilot boat appear.)

DAVID: There's the boat. *(He starts waving)* Over here, over here . . .

MABEL: Tell it to go away.

DAVID: It's too late now.

MABEL: I don't want to go.

DAVID: What are you talking about?

MABEL: Everything's perfect.

DAVID: But you're about to set a new world record. The first woman to swim from England to France.

MABEL *(Dully)*: The first woman to swim from England to France.

DAVID: Mabel Tidings!

MABEL *(Dully)*: Mabel Tidings.

DAVID: Well, aren't you excited? *(Pause)* Hello?

(Silence.)

MABEL *(Coming back to life)*: *Of course I'm excited, what do you take me for?!*

DAVID: That's more like it.

PILOT'S VOICE *(From the boat)*: You all set?

MABEL: All set.

DAVID: You're going to be brilliant.

MABEL: Don't take your eyes off me!

DAVID: Not for a second. And remember, let me know when you want something to eat or drink. I'll be right next to you in the boat.

MABEL: I will.

DAVID *(Kissing her)*: I miss you already.

MABEL: Until France.

DAVID *(Wades out to the boat and gets in)*: And beyond.

PILOT'S VOICE: Come on, Miss Tidings, you'd better get started while the tide's still with you. We've timed everything down to the second.

MABEL: I'm coming, I'm coming . . . *(She puts on her cap and goggles)*

DAVID *(From the boat)*: Good luck, M. T.

MABEL: Good luck to us all! ". . . and shot like a stone from a sling through the air, shouting and laughing with delight, head foremost, *she* plunges into the approaching wave!"

(Mabel takes a deep breath, shakes out her arms and legs and dives into the water. The curtain slowly falls.)

END OF PLAY

TINA HOWE spent her childhood and many happy adult summers swimming off the coast of Pride's Crossing. The water's not as clear as it used to be, but Little Misery and Greater Misery are still there. She is the author of *The Nest, Birth and After Birth, Museum, The Art of Dining, Painting Churches, Coastal Disturbances, Approaching Zanzibar* and *One Shoe Off.* Her awards include the New York Drama Critics Circle Award for Best American Play for *Pride's Crossing*, an OBIE for Distinguished Playwriting, an Outer Critics Circle award, a Rockefeller grant, two NEA fellowships, a Guggenheim fellowship, an Academy of Arts and Letters Award in Literature, and an American Theatre Wing award. In 1987, she received a Tony Award nomination for best play for *Coastal Disturbances.* She has been a visiting professor at Hunter College since 1990 and an adjunct professor at NYU since 1983. Ms. Howe is proud to have served on the council of The Dramatists Guild since 1990.